THE TRAVELING PSYCHOANALYST

To Marvin Osman
to join my journeys, and
find new adventures.
With my very best wishes

Larry Friedman

Los Angeles
November 1985

By the same author:

Psy'cho-a-nal'y-sis

The Traveling Psychoanalyst

BY
LAWRENCE J. FRIEDMAN, M.D.

INTRODUCTION BY
LUCY FREEMAN

PAUL S. ERIKSSON
MIDDLEBURY, VERMONT

© 1978 by Lawrence J. Friedman, M.D.
All rights reserved
Paul S. Eriksson, Publisher
Middlebury, Vermont 05753
George J. McLeod, Ltd., Toronto, Ontario
Printed in the United States of America

Library of Congress Catalog Card Number: 72-180305
ISBN 0-8397-8375-2

Photographs by the author

To
MARIANNE

CONTENTS

ILLUSTRATIONS

Following page 48

Shopping on Montmartre
Painter on Montmartre
M. Porisse with his little girl
Narrow street leading to the Cathedral in Chartres
In Obergrindelwald, Switzerland
Watching the mountain climbers
Mont Blanc — going straight up to Heaven
The glaciers of Mont Blanc — look like frozen turbulent rivers
Near the top of the Jungfrau
Wading in a rushing mountain creek in Tyrol
Drying hay in Vorarlberg
Spring in Switzerland

Following page 80

The Grossglockner, highest mountain in Austria
Above the glacier of the Grossglockner
Benedictine Monk and the Grossglockner
Hallstatt, Austria
The house Böck, our hotel in Hallstatt
Marianne in Hallstatt
Near Hallstatt
Hiking near Kitzbühel, Austria
Near Kitzbühel
On the high summer meadow
Sonje Fjord in Norway
Fisherman's lookout in Norway
Summer in Norway
The flower market in Bergen
Jeremiah by Max Band

INTRODUCTION

He travels most pleasurably who travels on the printed page with Dr. Lawrence J. Friedman. The rewards are of the highest: a literate, sensitive companion who provides a unique, enriching journey not only to far countries but into the far country of the human mind, which is Dr. Friedman's daily profession.

The author, a man of quiet brilliance, charisma and a deep sense of caring about his fellow man, takes us to Paris, Vienna, Rome, Budapest, Jerusalem, among other places, as he gives travel a new emotional dimension, one filled with startling insights as well as description. Dr. Friedman's personal philosophy, his wisdom, his zest for life, his ability to accept the pain, as well as the pleasure of living, he shares eagerly with the reader.

This is different from any travel book ever written. In the first place, who ever heard of a psychoanalyst writing a travel book? In the second place, Dr. Friedman is a psychoanalyst who knows how to write with style, with humor and with deep feeling. In the third place, it is a travel book that presents new discoveries about the human mind, for Dr. Friedman is not content merely to record what he sees in front of him but also shares what it stimulates in his imaginative, creative mind.

For instance, as he visits the Sistine Chapel, admiring the masterpieces of Michelangelo depicting man's fate from creation to damnation, he looks at the magnificent figure of God in the center of the ceiling. He thinks of how God helped "the first man" to perform the miracle of miracles, "to create from his own body, *to give birth to the first woman*, usurping the one function of the woman he is incapable of performing." Dr. Friedman theorizes, "The answer to this beautiful fantasy must be man's envy of woman's ability to create a new life and his resulting hostility to her," pointing out that "in the shortest time, she is depicted as the reason for man's downfall, for his being driven forever from paradise; she is pleasure-giving, necessary and the source of all evil."

Praise of Dr. Friedman's book has come from a variety of persons, including leading authorities in the mental health field:

"Your book is unique in my experience . . . so personal in a way which shares the little experiences with the big ones— each in a matrix of a broad point of view which relates us all to each other and the universe," says Dr. Joan Fleming.

"I feel your book is to be sipped, smelled, gently touched with a cat's tongue," writes Dr. David Tepper.

"This lovable book imparts an inner warmth . . . You have a passionate ability to enjoy life in its many variants," says Dr. Alexander Rogawski.

"There is in your book an unusual warm and personal tone, applied to a 'travelogue,' which makes it so different from everything else," says Dr. Fritz Redl.

"Fascinating, compulsive reading . . . awakens nostalgia and a kind of reminiscence in a reader who has never shared your experiences," says Dr. Lawrence Friedman (no relation to the author).

"This is a tremendous work in a very small compass; the biography of a civilization, as well as of the author and his beloved wife . . . a rare pleasure: a few hours with a cultivated man," says Dr. Henry Brosin.

And, from Dr. Robert (Hans) Jokl: "Your words are true because they are music and poetry, so rare in our prosaic time . . . your book uses analytic philosophy in a very positive sense, maybe more optimistically than justified, but with a deep belief in the improvability of the human mind . . . You are trying to explain that an ideal of balance and the beneficial use of aggression can be achieved, at least theoretically, and in our hearts and dreams."

This, from a travel book? Read on, and see.

Lucy Freeman

PREFACE

Some years ago a group of actors invited me to talk to them about psychoanalysis and literature. They belonged to a theatre group working on a new adaptation of Dostoyevsky's *Crime and Punishment*. Studying the life of Dostoyevsky, the background and meaning of the play, they had become intrigued with the concept of ambivalence—the interplay of love and hate—so prevalent in literature.

Our first encounter stimulated us all, prompting a series of informal sessions at my home, during which we explored the phenomenon of ambivalence—not only in literature, but in our lives as well, and in the shaping of civilization itself. We raised more questions than we had time to examine to our satisfaction, and it was this feeling of unfinished business—of questions unanswered—that made me want to write down experiences I have had, while living and traveling in many places. For these experiences have given me a perception of man's potential for love and hate and, in a broader sense, of the physical and emotional alternatives people possess for building or destroying, for experiencing pleasure or pain. I chose to put these thoughts in the form of "letters," thinking of it as a continuing dialogue with my actor-student group, and into a book for those others who might benefit from what I have learned.

Whether the episodes are funny or painful, purely personal or derived from history, art or literature, from the beautiful or the ugly, whether the letters are from Vienna, Paris, Rome, Budapest, or Jerusalem—they all illustrate ambivalence . . . the way I experienced it. The way millions have experienced it.

THE TRAVELING
PSYCHOANALYST

Paris

I. FLYING TO PARIS

It was late at night when our plane landed in Greenland, but the northern sun was shining as brightly as on a sunny day. Coming from California, I did not realize how cold it was until I noticed an American soldier driving a truck, pale and shivering in his fur-lined coat. In front of the terminal there was a tall pole with signs pointing to every part of the world—Paris, New York, Buenos Aires, Rome.... The largest sign simply read: "North Pole."

The flight was pleasant. The moment you leave the ground in an Air France plane, you are already in Europe—filled with excitement, reviving old memories and looking forward eagerly to new experiences. It still amazes me to leave the warm sunshine of Los Angeles and within a very few hours to be watching the floating icebergs, the fantastic colors and the glow of the midnight sun. By the time the second meal has been served, the plane is floating over the Eiffel Tower, the familiar landmark of Paris.

No matter how often we fly, I still can't take for granted the miracles of jet-age transportation. No problem for young people. Some years ago, on our first jet flight across the United States, my younger daughter, Lorraine, exclaimed: "Daddy, why does it take so long to get there?" I was amazed, but also glad, because the best we can hope for in raising our children is to help them learn how to adjust to the rapidly changing world they will have to live in.

Throughout history, one source of man's problems has been his inability to accept change, his anxiety-laden, tenacious clinging to the status quo, the known, the familiar. It is undoubtedly one of the reasons contributing to the periodic out-

3

breaks of violent upheaval which sweep away old orders and old beliefs.

We have come a long way from the primitive societies in which the course of life was predictable for generations. The times we now live in do not permit this luxury either for the individual or for society.

Of course all this has nothing to do with flying to Paris, but it forces one to realize how small the world has become. The Statue of Liberty is only a meal and a short nap away from the Eiffel Tower or from Big Ben! Jet transportation has brought people so close to one another that the fate of any man anywhere has become the immediate concern for all men everywhere.

II. LIBERTÉ, EGALITÉ, FRATERNITÉ

It has been a long time since I have written to you. I've just realized that I didn't answer your first letter and have only now read your second one. Don't take it personally—my unopened mail is increasing.

As often as I come to Paris, it always seems the same to me; alive and exciting. I feel impatient to stay in the hotel, to sleep, to spend time on anything except seeing Paris. It is certainly one of the most stimulating, beautiful cities in the world.

Our hotel is not the grandest, but it is pleasant, comfortable, a bit old-fashioned and superbly located. Several times now we have had the same rooms facing the court, away from the street—so quiet one can hardly believe to be in the center of this vibrant, surging, noisy world outside.

From one window, we can see into the kitchen of an apartment house where a young woman is preparing dinner. After a while, her husband arrives, bringing the inevitable bottle of wine and a long French bread fresh from the bakery.

Our other window overlooks the courtyard with its little fountain. The chestnut trees, just bursting into bloom, are old and tall, reaching up to our third floor windows. The same old man we have seen in other years slowly rakes the ground around the fountain. He works meticulously, as if it is important to him to erase any footsteps—to keep the little garden

4

free from human intrusion, preserving it exclusively for the bathing birds and the falling blossoms.

From the peace and quiet of our rooms, it takes only a short ride in our rickety little elevator or a run down three flights of stairs to be in the heart of Paris.

We can leave our hotel in two directions. One way is toward the Rue Saint Honoré, a narrow, busy street with many shops —one of them our favorite bakery, exuding the delicious odor of freshly baked bread, the window glowing with colorful fruit tarts. Presently, the streets widen, the traffic grows heavy, wildly confused and confusing. There are elegant stores, beautiful buildings, streets converging from every direction toward the Place de l'Opéra, one of my favorite haunts. Just to stand on any of its many corners or to sit at an outdoor table of the Café de la Paix, looking at the superb Opera House, the lovely trees on the boulevards, the thousands of passing cars, the excitable traffic cops, the animated pedestrians, is a sheer delight. A glass of Dubonnet or a cup of tea, and the hours slip by unnoticed. I never tire of the sight.

In the other direction from our hotel, we come upon an entirely different section of Paris: the Tuileries Gardens, the Louvre, the Place de la Concorde, the Seine. A short walk to the middle of the Tuileries and we are treated to one of the most breathtaking views in any city I have ever seen. Behind us, the great sweep of the Louvre. Before us, a limitless vista stretching across the beautiful flower gardens, across the Place de la Concorde, up the gently-rising Champs-Élysées and coming to rest in the far distance at the Arc de Triomphe in the Place de l'Etoile.

It is a sunny, warm spring day and the laughter of children at play is all around us. They run around the Gardens, race their sailboats on the large round pond, while old ladies bustle about, collecting rent for sitting on the chairs that encircle the pond.

We walk the length of the Tuileries toward the Place de la Concorde. The distance is great, but we move slowly, trying to stretch time—it is just too beautiful to hurry. Somehow, miraculously avoiding the thousands of cars running around

5

the magnificent fountains, we finally stand at the Obelisk in the middle of the Place de la Concorde, with new vistas to delight us. On the left bank of the Seine, the imposing Palais-Bourbon, which houses the National Assembly; ahead of us, the Church of the Madeleine with its many columns, built like a Greek temple. To it we make our way.

Who can leave the Madeleine without being drawn to the colorful flower stalls lining one entire side? Certainly not I—so we stop while I buy one of the fragrant, beautifully arranged bouquets Marianne loves so much.

Hours slip by; it is time to go home—our daughters will be waiting for us. We buy some cold cuts, a bottle of red wine, a couple of baguettes and flutes (different shapes of crisp French bread), a piece of freshly baked fruit tart with the fruit as artistically arranged and almost as colorful as the flowers, and we enjoy a delicious dinner.

After dinner, we all go to the Opéra-Comique, a delightful small theatre with good performances of classical operas. Then a stopover at a sidewalk cafe for a glass of Cointreau before we walk back to the hotel. We leave the children bedded down for the night and, too stimulated to sleep, we continue our walk to the Seine, and once again to the Place de la Concorde. The fountains are all lit up now, as are the great buildings and monuments. The whole scene glows and sparkles. The Champs-Élysées gleams red and white along its entire length from lights of the never-ending stream of automobiles.

There is a feeling I never lose in Paris, no matter how often I visit it. It is a peculiar sensation of loneliness, of being forever a stranger in this glittering, magnificent city. One can live here, enjoy everything it offers in beauty, in entertainment, in art, in culture, but one remains always a foreigner, always on the outside looking in. Actually, the feeling is more pleasurable than painful, contributing to a sense of unattached, unburdened freedom.

It was in the spring of 1927, that I came here for the first time, drawn to it by my long yearning for the city of my dreams and my desire to spend a few months with a friend of my childhood, who was studying medicine in Paris. Those

6

months come back to me whenever I return here—my little room on the second mansarde of the cheap students' hotel. An iron bed, two chairs, a small table, a few nails in the wall serving as a closet. The big window opening onto a balcony connecting a half-dozen other attic rooms—mansarde sounds so much nicer—. How vividly I remember sitting on this balcony on hot summer nights, listening to the music of a guitar, drinking *vin ordinaire*, eating smoked crevettes out of a paper bag, the heads of the crevettes "accidentally" falling into an open car below! A knock on my window early in the morning . . . someone asking for my binoculars in order to see the clock on the tower of the Gare du Nord. No one on the entire floor owned a watch!

I remember, too, the walks to the little clinic where my friend was in charge of the X-ray department . . . to the lectures at the Institute of Mme. Curie . . . or to listen to Pasteur Valery Radeau. It didn't matter how little one understood, it was good to listen to those great teachers or just to the sound of the beautiful language. On the way, stopping at a bistro for coffee and croissants and, whenever possible, making a small detour to drop in at Notre Dame. How enchanting it was in the early morning to feel the cool silence of this magnificent cathedral . . . to see an old woman kneeling before an altar lit by flickering candles . . . to be thrilled by the breathtaking colors of the stained glass windows illuminated by the rays of the morning sun.

Paris . . . center of so much beauty, so many art treasures created and collected throughout the centuries! But those centuries have also seen the other side of Man . . . his need to destroy, to torture, to kill . . . and certainly Paris has seen it all.

But to return to the present . . . It was very late last night when we found ourselves once again in the Place de la Concorde. The fountains, the public buildings with their massed tricolors, were no longer illuminated; the traffic no longer heavy; the Tuileries just a dark shadow. The wind was blowing a cold, misty rain, forcing the policemen under their rubber pelerines. Moving closer to one another, Marianne and I walked a little more briskly, silently holding hands.

Once again, I am carried back ... to the first time I walked here late at night, alone. There were few automobiles then. They moved with difficulty beween the slow, horse-drawn, two-wheel carriages which rumbled through the night, bringing fruits and vegetables to Les Halles. You do not see these any more, they have been replaced by heavy trucks; and very soon, Les Halles will be no more. But there were hundreds of them then—the same old carriages with their oversized wheels which brought the nobility of Paris, of all France, to this same magnificent Place de la Concorde to be executed day after day, month after month, by that ingenious invention of Dr. Guillotine. All this to the delirious joy of young and old, the children of the great French Revolution, chanting its slogan of "Liberté, Egalité, Fraternité"—which is still engraved on the public buildings of France.

It did not matter to the mobs whose head fell—that of the oppressor or the oppressed: the impotent Louis XVI or the exquisite Marie Antoinette; the playboy, the poet, the cultured, beautiful ladies, the expensive courtesans and, finally, the head of Robespierre, chief executioner, himself. The beat of the drums, the thud of the guillotine, the head dropping into the basket remained the same. After a while, saturated with the pleasure in violence, the crowds became smaller, the shrieks of joy quieter. France, in one of the seemingly unavoidable and violent convulsions of history, destroyed for generations much of her cultural and intellectual potential, a destruction from which the nation has never fully recovered. At the same time, France gave birth to the concept of man's equality, his drive for freedom and human dignity. . . .

By the time we arrived at our hotel, the rain was coming down quite heavily. With a last look at our sleeping children, we went to bed in our quiet room, wondering what they would find in Paris should they visit there decades from now.

III. MONA LISA

The drizzly rain the other night was colder than I thought. I woke up this morning with all the unpleasant symptoms of

8

a cold: stuffed head, runny nose, tickling throat and a rapidly disappearing voice. Impatient with my disability, I am tempted to ignore it but Marianne insists that I stay indoors and off my feet. I must resort to imagination to realize that I am still in Paris—assisted by the aroma of onion soup drifting in from a neighboring apartment and by the three-foot-long loaf of French bread and the fresh bouquet of spring flowers on our table.

Memories of my first visit crowd in again—the pleasant ones and the funny ones; most of the painful ones have faded away. I remember my first visit to the Louvre. My friend planned to make it a memorable and festive occasion. First we had breakfast at a sidewalk cafe, coffee with hot milk and all the croissants and brioches we could eat. He was looking forward eagerly to my reaction at seeing for the very first time that most famous of paintings, "Mona Lisa." Without a word, he led me through one room after another of the Louvre with its tremendous collection of treasures. He was practically holding his breath with expectation. What do you think happened? I felt ashamed for years at the memory of that first Sunday at the Louvre. Believe it or not, I went by the Mona Lisa without even noticing her. I am afraid her smile has never been the same since, and my friend never forgave me. He insisted that we turn back, but I hardly dared to look at the good lady. It was many years before I could do so without feeling guilty and ashamed, and I never could share the enthusiasm for her that most art lovers seem to feel. I wonder if many other people feel the same way but won't admit it!

The day, however, was not a complete loss. As we walked through the crowded halls and corridors, we suddenly came face to face with the "Venus de Milo," beautifully displayed, the magnificent white marble giving every appearance of vibrant life. I fell in love with that beautiful woman at first sight and my love and admiration have remained unchanged throughout the years. There is only one other work of art with the same overwhelming impact on me and that is Michelangelo's "Pietà" at Saint Peter's in Rome. Someday I'll tell you more about it.

9

IV. REFLECTIONS

Your pleasure with my glimpses of Paris makes my trip even more enjoyable. To share delightful experiences with others is very important to me. Although I can be alone, and have enjoyed many walks by myself, I prefer to be with someone even if we walk silently together. Which leads me to reminisce again.

After my first visit to Paris, two friends and I had planned to spend several weeks hiking in Switzerland before going back to Vienna. By the time we arrived in Geneva, however, one member of our party had to leave and a few days later, in Montreux, my other friend was hospitalized with acute appendicitis and I was left alone.

After six weeks of hiking, I had seen half of Switzerland. That was more than forty years ago, but I shall never forget the beauty of the trip and the warm friendliness of the farmers who provided me with food and with lodging in their haystacks during all those weeks. I also remember the loneliness, the frustration of having no one to talk to, to share the beauty with—to enjoy with me the snow-capped peaks sparkling in the sun and the mountainsides covered with symphonies of wildflowers. It is human nature to bear pain alone but to need company for full pleasure.

V. 1914 THE LAST TRAIN

You ask me about Europe of the 20's. Now is really the time to talk about it when, free from preoccupation with daily work and stimulated by the old environment, my mind can roam through the past, bringing back earlier experiences with all the vividness and intensity of the present.

Of course Europe of the 20's must have meant many different things to many people. Let me tell you what it meant to me, covering ten years of my life—from the beginning of manhood to graduation from medical school.

First I must go back a few years—1914, to the beginning of the First World War. Years of powerplay, conflict of interest,

10

political intrigue and blunders of the major European nations, like the Austro-Hungarian Empire, France, Germany and Russia, the war became inevitable. The murder of the Archduke Ferdinand of Austria in Sarajevo was the official reason and the final spark which ignited the holocaust engulfing Europe and the world for four long years. Even though the war ended in 1918, it had consequences which have never been solved and have been plaguing Europe ever since.

In the summer of 1942, at the beginning of my service in the Army of the United States, I was assigned to teach history to newly inducted troops. We were supplied with the official text for each lecture and you would not believe it, but 28 years later we were supposed to teach that *the reason* for the First World War was the Assassination of Archduke Ferdinand! That excuse was already corrected in textbooks when I was in high school. When I brought this to the attention of my commanding officer he replied: "Lieutenant, in the army you don't ask questions and don't give advice, you take orders. Medical officers are cheap and expendable." It took me a long time before I could fully appreciate his wise and honest advice.

The great enthusiasm of the first few days of the war quickly gave way to anxiety, and all the reassuring bulletins issued by the Government could not silence the mounting crescendo of approaching artillery, could not stem the swelling tide of wounded soldiers returning first by train, then by carriage and every other available transportation. Finally, with its forces in full retreat, it was no longer possible for the government of the Austro-Hungarian Empire to deny the breakthrough of the Russian Army on the Eastern borders of Hungary, and its rapid advance toward the city where I was born, many miles from this border.

How vividly I remember the panic and flight of the population of our city . . . the empty streets . . . the weirdly lit night sky accompanying the thunder of the approaching battle! My father did not panic easily, which of course kept us children also relatively unafraid. Finally, though, he decided that it was too dangerous for us to remain. Hurriedly, we boarded up

11

the doors and windows of our house in a naive attempt to keep out looters. On Yom Kippur, the holiest of the Jewish Holidays, we caught the last train leaving the city for the safety of Budapest, about 200 miles further in the interior. On the same train there was a famous orthodox rabbi from a neighboring city, as well as dozens of his devotees—none of whom, under any other circumstances, would have set foot in a moving carriage on a High Holy Day . . . or even on any Sabbath, of course. Candles burned and the chant of prayers mingled all day long with the cries of terrified children.

The train, crowded to the last inch, moved so slowly that one could keep up with it by walking alongside. On the outskirts of our city, we had to cross a broad, rain-swollen river and the rumor spread that the bridge had been mined. There were no Jews nor Gentiles on that train—no rabbis, no priests, no atheists, no young, no old, no friends, no enemies—just an agonized mass of human beings caught in one of the violent outbursts of man . . . expecting to be blown to bits but hoping against hope to live.

I will never forget those endless minutes as the long train slowly inched its way across the high bridge. There I stood, on an open platform, looking down into the muddy yellow water, clasping the hand of one my older sisters as if that could protect me from danger. After all these years, sometimes in nightmares, I can still feel the weight on my back of the wooden basket filled with food which each of us children were carrying, in case we might become separated or lost. I will never be able to forget the pain that clutched at my throat as the city of my birth, the bridge, the whirling river disappeared. How often I have re-lived that feeling! For years, whenever I boarded a train or plane leaving a loved one behind, I felt with fear that it was final, that I never would see the place and the one I loved again. And how many times it did happen! Each time engraving more deeply, more indelibly the picture of that bridge, that painful sense of loss, the face of a loved one never to be seen again. Perhaps that is why now I like to return to places where I have been before . . . to prove to myself that it does not have to be the last time!

12

VI. EUROPE OF THE 20'S

My last letter carried me far back into my childhood. Writing about those first experiences with the horrors of war made me realize again how deeply early childhood feelings and events influence our lives. They never lose their crucial impact, even when we think we have buried them forever. But to return to the Europe of the 20's.

The breakdown of the Eastern Front under the brunt of the Russian Revolution did not change the fortunes of the war. In 1918, the Central Powers, represented primarily by Germany and the Austro-Hungarian Empire, collapsed. With the exception of the United States, all the participants were totally exhausted. Four years of violence, destruction, bloodletting in a war which was supposed at best to last only a few months, undermined and destroyed centuries of order and tradition. England and the West European countries were capable of maintaining some continuity of identity, but the collapse of the vanquished was total. Destruction of industry, transportation, sources of food—disillusionment, hunger, large-scale starvation, epidemics of influenza, typhoid fever, breakdown of order, violence decimated the survivors, especially in the Eastern European countries.

The Communist Revolution in Russia spilled over into other parts of Europe. For a brief period it was established and maintained on a solid footing in Hungary under the leadership of Béla Kun. This created new violence and mobilized strong reactionary forces. Their teachings of hate dominated the atmosphere of Eastern Europe for decades.

You have undoubtedly learned a great deal about the post-World War I development of England, France, Italy, Germany; the Communist Revolution in Russia; the fate of President Wilson and the League of Nations; the ruthless, vengeful attitude of Clemenceau. The mistakes of those years have been used and misused to explain the horrors of the 30's in Europe and the breadlines in the United States. Above all, they made the even greater holocaust of the Second World War inevitable.

The schools in our country teach us less about Eastern Europe, where actions were initiated and changes effected

13

which have had far-reaching consequences for all of Europe. I am referring specifically to the dismemberment and consequent disintegration of which was then the Austro-Hungarian Empire. It consisted of an immense territory stretching from Bavaria and the Black Forest to the eastern limits of Transylvania, Bukovina and the Carpathian Mountains. It reached south to Trieste and to the shores of the Adriatic Sea. To the north it included Bohemia, Moravia, parts of Poland and extended all the way to the Russian border.

It was an autocratic monarchy, granting relative autonomy to the two largest groups—the Austrians and the Hungarians—and a somewhat less defined autonomy to the Czechs. Its borders included almost the entire length of the Danube, from its source in the Black Forest to the Iron Gate. Its political structure had not changed since 1848, following the unsuccessful, bloody uprising of the Hungarians for independence. It remained under the rule of Kaiser Franz Josef from 1848 until his death in 1916. Franz Josef was crowned Kaiser of Austria and King of Hungary. His permanent residence was in Vienna, although he recognized Budapest as the capital of Hungary and included in his Empire the ancient city of Prague.

In addition to the German-speaking Austrians and the Hungarians, the population of the Empire included a large number of other ethnic groups, speaking their own languages, living their own traditions and hating the two dominant powers. In the north, were the Czechs and the Sudeten Germans—who did not consider themselves Austrians—as well as the Poles, the Ruthenians of the Tatra Mountains, the Russians, the large communities of Rumanians in Transylvania, sprinkled with islands of Germans. In the south, were the Serbs, the Croatians, the Montenegrans. They represented almost pure ethnic cultures at their centers but were inevitably mixed on their borders and they mistrusted and hated each other even more, if possible, than they hated their masters. They spoke different languages, barely communicating with each other and belonged to different religions ... an additional source of prejudice.

The dominant, official religion was Roman Catholic. How-

14

ever, there was a large Protestant movement in Hungary and most of the Slavic groups belonged to the Greek Orthodox Church. If there was any common meeting ground for these differing cultures it was their intense anti-Semitism towards the millions of Jews within the borders of the Empire. The sophisticated anti-Semitism of Viennese high society, and the more vulgar forms common to its burghers, were nurtured and exploited for political purposes from Innsbruck to Zagreb, from Prague to Budapest to Sarajevo—from the halls of the universities to the mud huts of the superstitious, bigoted, illiterate peasants.

Anti-Semitism found expression all the way from social ostracism and exclusion from many professions in the higher cultural centers and big cities of the west to periodic bloody pogroms in the hamlets and villages of the eastern sectors of this far-flung Empire. Anti-Semitism forced large segments of the Jewish population to live in ghettos, huddled among themselves, clinging ever more tightly to their own heritage as the only way of safeguarding their religious, cultural and physical safety; increasing and perpetuating their own fears and prejudices against outsiders. Prejudice, alas, is not the prerogative of any one race, color or religion!

Which reminds me of my first day in U.S. Army uniform in 1942. I was standing on a street corner in a small Texas town. An old black man in tattered clothes, his toes sticking out of wornout shoes, turned to me and said: "Lieutenant, you know what we do after this war? The first thing we do, we kill all the Jews." Through misty eyes, visualizing the marching Nazi hordes, I replied: "You're right, Pop, you're right." I didn't have the heart to deprive him of his illusion that even he, in his miserable existence, could be superior to someone, could have the power to hurt someone.

But to return to the Empire. It had culture, tradition, famous centers of learning. It formed a connecting link between the Occident and the Orient, with one hand reaching into the heart of Western civilization and the other deep into the Balkans. The racing Orient Express symbolized its connection with the isolated, mysterious countries of the Middle East. Its

15

Eastern border was the gateway for the conquering hordes of Ottomans who were stopped from overrunning all of Europe in 1683 only at the walls of Vienna.

Within its own borders the Empire had everything needed for economic well being: navigable, life-giving rivers, mountains full of minerals, the endless plains of central Hungary to provide unlimited supplies of food, the fabulous forests of the east, herds of cattle and sheep and, as we know today, deposits of oil, potentials for power development, uranium, outlets to the ocean — everything a country could possibly require for centuries of growth.

Everything, that is, except the ability of its ruling class to understand any human needs beyond food and shelter, the minimum physical necessities of life. They never understood the hunger for human dignity, for freedom of thought and action, the need to at least hope for a better life, if only in dreams. Has any tyrant, whether individual or state, ever understood this? Has history ever taught them what our psychological studies of man make so clear today — that the greater the pressure, the longer it is maintained, the more resentment, anger and hatred are kept under forced control — the greater will be the reaction, the more violent the retribution?

The masters of the Austro-Hungarian Empire knew all too well how to use pressure to subjugate the masses decade after decade, generation after generation. I have seen the whip of an arrogant young Hungarian officer slash the face of a terrified Rumanian peasant because he did not understand a command in a foreign tongue. I have seen rifle butts brutally striking men in the presence of their wives and children.

None of the inhabitants of this Empire, with the exception of the Austrians, ever considered themselves citizens of a unified country, but minorities in a dangerous environment. The Austrians tolerated the Hungarians and treated all the other minorities as serfs without rights, offering no recourse for their grievances, keeping them illiterate, subjecting them to scorn, to untold cruelties and servitude. Perhaps it would have been impossible to achieve a national identity for this conglomerate of so many ethnic groups even with the greatest understanding and effort; perhaps man's fear and intolerance of all who look a little different, speak a different language, worship a different God is too great to overcome. In any case, it was never even attempted here.

Looking back, one wonders that the Empire lasted as long as it did. No one will ever know how many of the cocky young officers were killed, not by the enemy but by shots from their own ranks, giving expression to the resentment and hate of generations.

When, after the war, the collapse came, it was total. I watched Hungarian soldiers as they spat on and stamped into the mud the proud *Doppeladler,* the two-headed eagle of the Habsburgs; the barefoot army of the newly-created, larger Rumania beating their Hungarian oppressors, killing the children, raping the women, looting and burning their homes. It was only two years earlier that I had seen the endless ranks of helmeted German cavalry moving west, their horses loaded with the spoils of looted Rumanian homes. The Rumanian looters, moving in the opposite direction, were not as well dressed; they wore any uniform they could find; they were rowdy, less disciplined and their hatred was uncontrollable, subdued only temporarily in periodic alcoholic stupors.

The same things were happening in the north, west and south. The Austro-Hungarian Empire fell apart like a poorly put-together puzzle. Some parts were annexed by the victors of the war — South Tyrol by Italy, Transylvania by Rumania. Some of the northeastern sections went to Russia. Poland, Austria, Hungary, Czechoslovakia became separate states; Yugoslavia was newly created. Only two of the independent states, Austria and Hungary, ended up as homogeneous ethnic groups with a common language—German in Austria, Hungarian in Hungary (except for some scattered pockets of Germans).

Look at the others. South Tyrol, inhabited almost entirely by Austrians speaking only German and hating the Italians — a powder-keg with a short fuse constantly erupting in violence. Yugoslavia, encompassing various nationalities who had been murderous enemies for centuries. Rumania which to this day

17

persecutes the Hungarians within its borders even more fiercely than the Hungarians persecuted them before 1918. Czechoslovakia, a mixture of Czechs, Slavs, Sudeten Germans, Hungarians, Ruthenians, Rumanians, Russians—speaking their various languages, hating each other with passion.

Economically, too, the formerly well-balanced unit fell apart. There was Austria, the blown-up head of the Empire, left without food and with its industry deprived of its former market in the eastern agricultural areas of the Empire. There was Hungary, which had been the breadbasket for the entire Empire without any appreciable industry of its own — without coal, wood, energy potentials — reduced to using wheat for fuel at a time when a loaf of bread in Vienna was at a premium. Rumania, with the annexation of Transylvania, suddenly grew to unnatural proportions, struggling with the highest rate of illiteracy, a lack of skilled industrial workers, teachers, civil servants, professionals of any kind. Burdened by its feudal backwardness, Rumania was unable for decades to utilize its great natural resources. It brings to mind the chaos and helplessness of some of the newly-emerging African nations.

Yugoslavia was not much better off. Czechoslovakia was the only state with an almost balanced economy of industry, agriculture, natural resources, educational facilities and a trained force of civil servants. For many years, its government was fairly liberal and tolerant toward its minorities. Czechoslovakia therefore developed far beyond all the others and received the greatest loyalty and support from its polyglot population. Hungary, Rumania, Yugoslavia, on the other hand, struggled during the aftermath of the war through violent upheavals ranging from one extreme to another, from suppressive Fascist dictatorships to monolithic Communism. They have not achieved economic independence to this day.

A little economic cooperation between these separate states could have made the existence of each tolerable and could have led to successful growth in a few years. Instead, the long oppression, the irrepressible hatred of the minorities toward each other, led to an exaggerated nationalism. Borders were closed to practically all commercial and cultural exchange.

Even travel from one country to another was viewed with suspicion and subjected to endless red tape, making bribery of officials a universal practice which exposed one to personal peril. Even today, in spite of their Communist governments, travel between Hungary, Rumania and Czechoslovakia is more difficult than between Hungary and Austria.

It is painful to note that the one common denominator attributable to all these new nations, large and small, with their divergent national characters, economic and cultural status and changing forms of government, was their anti-Semitism. Their persecution of Jews in one form or another—depending on their cultural sophistication or lack of it—continued and grew, from Vienna to Baku, from Prague to Bolzano, from Budapest to the mountains of Montenegro.

The intensity of their anti-Semitism became even more aggravated during the 20's, with the worsening of economic conditions, and reached its cataclysmic peak in the 30's with the advent of Hitler. The Germans, with their efficient organization and pseudo-scientific propaganda, systematically exploited the existing prejudice and hatred. Ultimately, Hitler and the self-appointed representatives of the "master race" arrived at their "final solution of the Jewish question" — the methodical extermination of the Jews of Europe, including the millions of helpless victims living in the remnants of the old Austro-Hungarian Empire.

By now it must be obvious to you that the disintegration of this Empire was inevitable once it was put under severe and prolonged pressure. There have been other nations which have suffered violent upheavals, lost wars, had bloody revolutions —like France, Russia, Germany—but they did not lose their national identity; they did not disintegrate. Sometimes adversity even reaffirmed their identity. The Austro-Hungarian Empire was not a nation—it had no identity. It had to fall apart.

The lust for revenge, the short-sightedness of the Grand Alliance not only promoted this disintegration but encouraged the fortification of the borders of hate. By creating artificial boundaries, they perpetuated provocation and strife among the new nations. They awarded territories inhabited exclusively by

19

one ethnic group or another to their mortal enemies. Economic units, villages, farms, even family structures were split apart. Because of their fear of the historic power of the Empire it did not occur to them that even if politically divided, encouragement and promotion of economic cooperation between the new states would have served the interest of all Europe. Economic health could have been the best bulwark against the eastward expansion of the Third Reich, instead of whetting its megalomanic fantasies of world domination. It could have been the bulwark against the westward march of Communism, as it was for so long the bulwark against the Ottoman hordes invading Europe from the East.

What happened in the Europe of the 20's, what happened in the country where I was born and spent my childhood determined the future of every member of my family and of most of my friends. Very shortly after the First World War, the members of my immediate family were divided up among four countries on a constant war footing with each other—frequently making even correspondence impossible for months on end, for fear of censorship and reprisals. Little did I dream then, that in less than two decades, instead of being separated into four countries by artificial boundaries we would be divided by oceans and living on four different continents.

During those years, I also had a friend—the kind of friend so important in the life of an adolescent. This friendship lasted throughout my youth and adulthood, only to end recently—as a direct result of the events of the early 20's.

VII. MY FRIEND

In my last letter, I mentioned a friend whose fate was also determined by the convulsions of the 20's. Let me tell you about him. I met him originally in one of those cultural clubs which were so significant a part of our lives as high school students. At 16, he was a year my senior, a newcomer to our city from a smaller town about 30 miles away. Our club of upper-class students from different schools was primarily interested in literature. Familiarity with modern literature—practically banned in our conservative school system—was a

20

prerequisite for membership. The club was also dedicated—without announcing it officially—to the study and dissemination of the works of the classical Hungarian writers, prohibited by the Rumanian authorities.

As time went on, it became one of the many organizations of young Hungarians dreaming and planning for a time when the greatness of Hungary would be restored, when we would defeat and destroy the barbaric, illiterate, despised Rumanian conquerors. Our nationalistic orientation was centered around one of the greatest of the Hungarian poets, Petöfy, the spiritual hero of the 1848 uprising against the Austrian oppressors, and around Ady, a modern poet representing the avant garde.

Ady spent most of his life in Paris, where he wrote his beautiful poetry, especially appealing to imaginative adolescents. Both poets were rebels—Petöfy oriented toward the past, Ady away from it. They were ideal figures for youngsters struggling toward maturation to identify with—one pulling us back to the past, to conservatism, to childhood, and fatherland and mother-tongue; the other propelling us toward the new, the adventurous, the forbidden, the strange . . . all summed up in the vision of Paris.

Paris symbolized the ideal of freedom, the center of culture, city of artists, writers, Bohemians. Notre Dame, the Louvre! Paris was also Montmartre with its apaches and intriguing prostitutes, its Moulin Rouge and Folies-Bergères. Above all, Paris was the home of Balzac, Dumas, Proust, Zola and Anatole France; of Toulouse-Lautrec and Rodin and all the other greats we pictured walking the windswept boulevards so beautifully evoked by Ady, as were furtive characters in dark streets selling pornographic pictures of *les quarante-deux positions de l'amour*.

The friend of whom I speak would recite the patriotic poems of Petöfy with the same fervor as those of Ady, with their moody and haunting cadences. We also shared an interest in the imaginative and the intriguing backstage life of the theatre. At sixteen, I wrote some second-rate reviews for our local theater. The impulse to create literature was less urgent than my desire to gain the attention of a very attractive young

21

actress. I must confess I was not very successful. Her ability did not match her looks and my literary talent lagged behind my admiration and my ambition to promote her.

My friend and I became inseparable, seeing each other daily in our homes, since we attended different schools. We often dined out together—eating in restaurants at that age and in that environment was unusual and quite a status-symbol.

The forty-odd members of our club all left Rumania after graduation from high school, if not before. Because of the severe anti-Semitism and restrictions of the *numerous clausus* in the Hungarian universities, the majority ended up in Padua, Paris or Vienna, the three great havens for the victims of intellectual persecution at that time. My friend went to Paris to study medicine while I pursued my medical studies in Vienna.

During the next few years we saw each other only during summer vacations at home, spending practically all our time together. We had long discussions about our lives, thoughts, feelings, plans, successes, failures, the pleasures and pains of our increasingly meaningful relationships with women. We exchanged experiences with other friends home on vacation, invented and listened to tall stories nobody believed. We told each other everything in order to share and clarify our feelings and our struggles. We were competitive, of course, proud and jealous of each other at the same time, and underwent every phase of the ambivalent attraction so characteristic and so helpful in the friendships of late adolescents, all trying to find direction, to establish the identity of their approaching manhood.

At the end of each summer, we returned to our respective universities, exchanging long letters frequently. My friend's letters only served to quicken my desire to see Paris and, in 1927, after completing my first group of examinations, I finally got there for the first time. Because no place can ever live up to the daydreams and expectations of an adolescent, there were disappointments of course. Nevertheless, that visit was one of the most wonderful experiences of my young life.

By this time, we were both more mature, had less need of

each other and had independent interests. He was busy preparing for examinations while working at a full-time job. I
was devoting my days and most of my nights, too, to exploring
Paris. An occasional telephone call or a hurried lunch at a
cheap bistro were our main contacts during the week, but we
usually spent Sundays together. When it came time to leave,
our farewells were as warm as ever, but they were farewells
of two adults—who remained friends but no longer served the
same needs they had shared during adolescence.

The next summer was the last one we both spent at home.
Political pressures, augmented by our refusal to interrupt our
studies for years of military service in the hated Rumanian
Army, made our visits dangerous. It was 40 years ago that I
saw the city of my birth for the last time. From then on, the
homes of my married sisters in Hungary and Czechoslovakia
became the rendezvous for family reunions.

My correspondence with my friend became increasingly
sporadic. Years later in 1935 on my way to the United States,
he met me at the railroad station in Paris. By that time he was
professionally and financially quite successful, published a
number of scientific papers and a charming biography of a
great man in medical history.

We talked for about an hour in my hotel room; he apologized
for not inviting me to stay with him, hoping that I would be
more comfortable in a hotel. He said goodby awkwardly with
the excuse of having an important engagement for dinner.

The next morning I left Paris for LeHavre, to board the
S.S. Normandie on my way to the United States.

In the next few hours our majestic ship passed the massed
armada of the French fleet. Their power emphasized the
danger of the impending Spanish Civil War. It increased my
feelings of loneliness but it was not my friend's face that was
following me. It was the image of someone else looking at me
from the haze of the darkening horizon, from the churning,
glimmering waves, the bottomless depth of the Atlantic. It was
the motionless figure of a slender young woman standing alone
in the crowd in Vienna, watching my train slowly pulling out
from the *Westbahnhof*. Tears frozen in deep dark eyes, held

back by courage and by the conviction of the inevitability of it all, and a hardly visible smile of encouragement on her kind face. No stranger would have seen the pain clutching at her throat, the faithful courageous heart beating against her chest, the quivering knees hardly capable of holding her up. Only I saw it, knew it, felt it in the vibration of the ship crossing the Atlantic and in the struggles of the following painful years of separation.

Since then my friend and I exchanged a few letters, saw each other once and probably for the last time a couple of years back. I wrote to him at the close of the war, after the nightmare of the German occupation, and again on our visit to Paris ten years later. The letters did not come back, neither did I receive any reply.

The reason seemed obvious, as with so many of the others who perished, but I would not give up. After hours of looking in telephone directories of Paris and vicinity, and with the enthusiastic help of the telephone operator at our hotel, I found him.

Accompanied by a charming teenaged daughter, he was at our hotel as quick as he could, insisting we go to his home in one of the small towns near Paris. Our plans being definite for our flight to the States the next day, we could not accept.

By the time the evening was over, we realized it was good that we had not and we knew that most probably this was our last meeting.

As an officer in the French Army, he was wounded at Dunkirk, receiving a hero's decoration and reception. Years before the war, in order to overcome the mistrust of the French toward foreigners and in order that his children should not repeat our experiences, he succeeded in convincing the people where he lived, practiced and had become an influential citizen that he was a native Frenchman. Accepting all the religious and cultural customs of his environment, it seemed he had found a method for an orderly and secure life until one day, during the Nazi occupation, a horde of French storm troopers stopping one of the trains of the Metro, ordered all males to strip, to pick out the Jews. (Gentiles in general were not circumcized in Europe.) Somehow he escaped, hiding in Southern France during the rest of the Nazi horror.

My visit to his home might have given away his secret, which he had just recently shared with his grown up children. The enthusiasm of our first meeting after so many years came to nothing.

There was some pain, and there still is some faint echo of it—knowing that he is only a telephone call away—but no anger, no resentment. He was the most meaningful, most important friend of my life.

You see all this had a lot to do with the Europe of the 20's: the beginning, the course, and the end of this story.

Many of our friends perished in the holocaust of the last war. He had to bury himself alive and continue to live.

VIII. PARIS, 1927

Since my last letter, we have enjoyed a delightful performance of *Rigoletto* at the Opéra and an unforgettable evening with Marcel Marceau, the great pantomimist. We had of course seen him in person and on television at home and he was great, but in his own environment and his own small theatre so perfectly suited to his requirements, the experience was all the more satisfying.

The Opéra in Paris is one of the most beautiful opera houses I have ever seen and even if the performances do not always rank with those in some of the other great opera houses of Europe, it is always a pleasure to go there. The Grand Staircase, the Grand Foyer, the whole magnificent interior contribute to one's enjoyment of the performance.

For me, opera ranks among the highest forms of artistic achievement. The union of drama and music, of instruments and the human voice, which can be more beautiful than any instrument, is to me beyond comparison. Even with average voices, half-good acting and a reliable orchestra, I find it pleasurable.

In my student years, the Paris Opéra was very elegant. For most performances, black tie was obligatory in the parterre and loge seats and, on some special occasions, even white tie.

People also dressed for many night clubs. For a student who wanted to see the night life of Paris, when he had barely enough money to make ends meet, a tuxedo was an absolute necessity. Anyone who had a tuxedo (and I had one made for my graduation from high school) could use it, lend it to friends or rent it out to other students and thereby gain admission to all the good night clubs without charge.

Night clubs welcomed students, if formally dressed, to fill up the empty tables—especially during the early evening hours; it improved the atmosphere. We could watch the floor shows, even dance. Some clubs actually put a bottle of cheap wine on our table; others parted only with mineral water. It was understood that as soon as paying guests needed a table, we would be asked very discreetly to leave. There were nights when we made the rounds of several clubs, seeing some of the best shows, staying anywhere from a few minutes to an hour. Usually, long before midnight—free tables no longer available—we would be on the Métro, returning to our homes in the Quartier Latin. There were other nights, generally on weekends, when it was impossible to get in anywhere, but we could at least promenade around the nightclubs of Montmartre or Montparnasse dressed in our best. Occasionally we would be invited to join people who could afford it and enjoyed the company of students.

The kind of dating customary in America, where young men pay all the expenses when they date a girl, was unknown in Europe, at least at that time. However, my tuxedo and I had a lot of fun together and between me and my friends, it led a busy life during those months in Paris.

IX. MARIE BONAPARTE

If it is true for any profession that periodically one has to get away from it, it is certainly true for psychoanalysis. The intense preoccupation with the needs of others, day after day, month after month—the enforced emotional and physical passivity—can be exhausting and disturbing for the analyst, his family and his work. Some physical activity and some outside interests are absolutely essential. Some analysts swim for relaxation, some take walks, some go to a gym. Many of them develop interests in various activities—theatre, music, social problems, lecturing, teaching—and I, as you know, besides all other activities, love to travel.

But even though I am remote from psychoanalytic concerns at the moment, I could not leave Paris without paying tribute to Marie Bonaparte, Princess of Greece and Denmark, one of the first of the French psychoanalysts and for many years a leading spirit in the movement.

She was an outstanding scientist, a great humanitarian and a gracious and wonderful human being. It was mainly through her efforts and personal influence that Freud and his family were permitted to leave Vienna after the German occupation, and that they were saved from destruction in a Nazi horror camp. If she had never done anything else in her life, the world would owe her eternal gratitude for this alone.

I met her for the first time in London, at the centennial celebration of Freud's birth, in May 1956. The ceremonies took place in the house where Freud lived and died after leaving Vienna and which has remained the home of his daughter and scientific heir, Anna Freud. Brief as was my personal acquaintance with her, it was sufficient to win my great respect and liking. I saw her for the last time in 1961, at the International Congress for Psychoanalysis in Edinburgh. She died in Paris at the age of 84, shortly after a futile flight to California to intercede for Caryl Chessman—who had been sentenced to the gas chamber many years before—and to save the sovereign state of California from the disgrace of his execution. She was devoted all her life to the fight against brutality, to the struggle for human dignity. The failure to prevent Chessman's execution was a grievous disappointment to her.

She will never be forgotten by those who were privileged to know her, however slightly, and she will be esteemed by all the coming generations of psychoanalysts.

X. MONTMARTRE, PLACE DU TERTRE

Since this will be my last letter from Paris, I will devote it to describing our visits to Montmartre with its artist colony, its Place du Tertre and Basilica du Sacré-Coeur—landmarks I would no more neglect on a trip to France than I would neglect drinking French wine or eating French bread.

Our first visit was unexpectedly brief. We had rented a car —a brand new Peugeot 404—and the drive was a short one, but the cobblestone streets leading up to the top of the hill are steep. When we got there, we were immediately surrounded by a crowd of gesticulating Frenchmen motioning us to get out of the car quickly. We did. Our radiator was boiling. We waited for it to cool off, then coasted down and spent most of the day looking for the rental company's garage. By the time we found it and the repairs were made, the day was spent.

Driving around Paris is no mean undertaking. The congestion is unbelievable. Thousands of cars driving at breakneck speed through narrow, winding streets, endangering the lives of pedestrians on foot-wide sidewalks. They race along boulevards, four-six-eight abreast in a ceaseless stream, so that it is almost impossible to cross on foot. In the great squares, the confusion is indescribable as they cut across each other, oblivious of danger, in order to get in or out of six, eight, even twelve converging streets.

There are traffic signals and regulations and there are policemen. Ah, those policemen! Violently gesticulating without pause, their only function seems to be to urge you to drive on, drive fast, don't slow down—just go . . . go . . . make room for the thousands of cars behind you. Above all, never stop, for whatever reason. Add to this the innumerable, unexpected one-way streets with no parking space anywhere in sight and driving, for anyone who is not completely at home in the city, is an exciting adventure but does not make for efficient transportation. This is true for practically every large city in Europe. Since they were built centuries before the advent of automobiles, many of their cobblestone streets though picturesque are too steep and narrow even for horse-carriages.

On any journey, some rain of unhappiness must fall. This was our day! By the time we got back to our hotel, Marianne and the children were in tears, justifiably angry and thoroughly disgusted with me. They put their feet down firmly—no more driving around Paris. The Métro was good enough for them. Even though I did not admit it right then and there, they were right, of course.

Today, good friends again, we waved a disdainful goodbye to our car, took the Métro to the Place de l'Opéra and walked from there to Montmartre. Although it is at least an hour's walk, there is so much to see along the way that the time just flew. First, the Grand Boulevard Haussmann with its great department stores, then the narrow streets with their little shops and apartment houses, the Moulin Rouge, and up through the winding Rue Lepic, the market street.

There is something fascinating about the way stores display their wares in Paris. Everything is on the street—bookstalls on the Left Bank, miscellaneous merchandise at the entrances to the department stores and above all, foods. Here on the Rue Lepic are stalls of vegetables, fish, meat, flowers, bedspreads and yardage, clothing and underwear and just about everything else you can think of. You might very well fancy yourself somewhere in the Orient! At first it may strike one as strange, but the traveler to other Mediterranean countries quickly discovers that this is common practice—from Spain to France, Italy, the Balkans, Greece, Turkey, Egypt and Israel—a connecting link between Europe and the Orient.

On hot days, your nose guides you from afar to the fish vendor or the butcher's stall. Most Americans, with their exaggerated sense of hygiene, are shocked by the total lack of concern for sanitation. They are convinced that anyone eating these foods, sampled by so many flies, will be sure to contract some dreadful disease. Perhaps so, but it's a great sight.

We continued to walk slowly up the increasingly steep streets, past smaller and smaller hotels and apartment houses with dark foyers and narrow, winding stairs leading four and five flights up into dingy apartments inhabited mainly by artists young and old, successful and unsuccessful. The ubiquitous laundry waves in the breeze, from every window and balcony. In every block there are several small restaurants, just large enough to hold a bar and two or three tables dressed in checkered tablecloths. Several men stand about, aperitif or beer in hand. Some look like all-day-and-night guests with weather-beaten Basque berets on their heads, scarves around the neck and cheap brown cigarets glued to the lips of unshaven faces.

Finally, we arrived in the funiculair, the cable car which takes you to the top of Montmartre. Next to it are the steep steps the children use to run up, the adults to walk down. Or you can walk all the way to the top through streets circling the Butte of Montmartre and leading to the Place du Tertre and the Basilica of the Sacré-Coeur.

The Sacré-Coeur is a church of peculiar architecture. From a distance it looks like a combination of a Russian church without the onion on top and a conglomeration of elongated Byzantine cupolas. It is built of white stone and would look more natural on a hill in Istanbul. Missing only are a slender minaret and a *muezzin* calling Mohammedans to greet the rising sun and attest to the glory of Allah. In spite of its bizarre shape, or perhaps because of it, Sacré-Coeur is as famous a landmark of Paris as is the Madeleine or Notre Dame. One cannot visualize Montmartre without it, and more brushes have been worn out painting it than perhaps any other build-ing in the world.

Our favorite haunt is the little square at the very top—enclosed by small buildings, their facades painted in a variety of colors: weatherbeaten red, blue, gray and yellow. Each houses a restaurant or cabaret, its garden extending into the middle of the square. All around, busily working on their palettes are dozens and dozens of painters—beardless young ones and bearded, long-haired veterans of every nationality. Hovering over them in a continuous procession are the crowds of tourists from every part of the world—looking, criticizing, advising and bargaining for the hundreds of oils, gouaches, watercolors, ink and pencil drawings displayed on the ground, on stands, benches and on all the walls not already plastered with advertisements for Dubonnet, Napoleon brandy and the half-naked girls of the famous cabarets.

By the time we arrived at this square after our leisurely walk, it was time for lunch and we were hungry. The artists were sitting about, some munching on sandwiches or candy; others, joined by wives and children, partaking of hot food direct from their own kitchens. One unforgettable sight—an apparently well-to-do artist enjoying a feast on the front seat of his almost-new Citroen. Seat covered with a spotlessly white cloth, china, silver, napkin and wineglass correctly placed, an assortment of appetizing dishes and a bottle of red wine—as orderly and proper as if he were being served in a restaurant of quality.

On our many visits throughout the years, we have sampled the various restaurants but we increasingly prefer the sandwiches prepared by a nearby delicatessen. Our favorite is a foot-long sandwich of French bread filled with sliced hard-cooked eggs and tomatoes. For those whose gums have become sore from the daily enjoyment of this crisp-crusted bread, a bag of *pommes frites* and a hot *saucisson* (just plain hot dog, usually of horsemeat) would be better. Whichever you choose, you can sit down with it at any one of the sidewalk cafes, order a drink—wine, beer, aperitif or, of course, Coca Cola—and enjoy your lunch in style.

The influx of American soldiers and tourists after the last war has made chewing gum, hamburgers and hot dogs available everywhere. Nothing, however, compares with the popularity of Coca Cola. You see the name everywhere you go: in tremendous neon lights on the Place de l'Opéra, in all French cafes and in the cafes of all the other countries; in the beer-halls of Vienna, the catacombs on the Appian Way, at the top of Mont Blanc and among the ruins of Pompeii. America's greatest post-war conquest abroad must be the Coca-Colanization of Europe.

Yesterday, having bought milk at the delicatessen, we did not patronize a cafe but took our lunch to the edge of the hills where, sitting on the remaining wall of a torn down building, in the shade of a chestnut tree, we could enjoy our repast while feeding on one of the most spectacular views of Paris. At one glance it encompassed the Eiffel Tower, the Seine, Notre Dame, the Opéra, the Tuileries, the Hotel des Invalides where Napoleon lies, and even my favorite clock on the Gare du Nord.

On a nearby bench, having finished his meager lunch, an old man dozed. He looked like one of those tragic figures one sees so frequently on Montmartre, an artist who may have come there decades ago full of hope, full of ambition, but who never made it. Yet, they cling to Montmartre, could not bear to live anywhere else. For better or worse, this is their only world.

After lunch, we returned to the Place du Tertre, joining the afternoon crowd grouped behind one painter or another. Whenever we come here, we buy pictures. On their very first visit, we had told our children that they could buy whatever they liked. They were highly pleased and went off to search for their first paintings. It didn't take them long. Each fell in love with one just being painted. They watched for hours while the artists completed their treasures, then proudly and carefully carried the wet oils back to our hotel.

Barbara chose a painting of a little church in Normandy (painted in memory of his mother by a middle-aged M. Gebhard) using only black, red and white, his Madonnas having an almost sculpture-like, three-dimensional quality. Lorraine bought a colorful sketch of a flower-girl standing behind her cart on a corner of the Rue Lepic, this one the creation of a young man named M. Pac.

Marianne and I selected one depicting the narrow street leading up to the corner of the square where the restaurant of Mére Catherine stands. By this time, it was late afternoon and its shadows lent a razor-sharp outline to the trees in the painting, the colorfully dressed women, the ever-present pair of policemen with their pillbox hats, carefully folded blue pelerines and white sticks. All in all, not a great painting but we enjoy it because the color photo-like quality of it evokes so vividly the many happy hours we have spent on Montmartre. Our choice was also influenced by our delight in the artist, M. Porisse, a charming young father whose four-month-old baby girl in her carriage remained beside him during the whole afternoon.

Before we left, we also bought several small watercolors by a young man who signed himself by the name of Gui. These are little gems, scenes of Montmartre's steep streets with their hundreds of steps leading the eye to the overpowering view of Paris from the top of the hill.

I have seen other places with artists and their paintings, in other parts of Paris, in other cities, on the streets or in galleries, but there is only one Montmartre and one Place Du Tertre. It is not just the Place, but one which always seemed genuine to me. Many painters worked there throughout its history. Some were great talents, who became famous, their pictures worth fortunes—even if not during their lifetime,—the majority were mediocre; others without any ability. But whether great or small, gifted or without any talent, they were sincere in their efforts, in contrast to many of the artist's centers of our time.

By the time we reluctantly descended in the funicular, it was evening. The city resembled an ocean reflecting a myriad of stars and the famous landmarks looked like so many illuminated pleasure boats on a moonlit, exotic night.

Vichy

XI. THE SHOW CALLED "OUR LIFE"

My sarcastic remark about the exaggerated concern of American's with sanitation was premature. Here I am in Vichy, recovering from a short but miserable illness named "turista" which afflicts so many Americans on visits to Mexico.

We left Paris ten days ago in our fine new Peugeot—early in the morning to avoid the rush. Heading south took us out of the city fast, and the French highways are among the best to drive in Europe. Well marked, not crowded and, unless you get caught behind a loaded hay cart on a narrow road, you make very good time.

We had planned to visit the Chateau country on the Loire but something was urging me in the opposite direction, to the town where the friend of my youth had settled. I had no intention of visiting him, I just wanted to see the place and to bid a silent farewell to the relationship. We lunched at an outdoor restaurant in the main square, facing the inevitable cathedral. It was a typical small French town that one would drive through without a second glance. Interesting to reflect that, far from his birthplace and in a foreign land, he had established his life again in a place identical in many ways with the one he had left at age 16, the one he had had to reject and deny in his adult life.

Late that afternoon we were approaching Chartres. Long before there is any sign of the city, like a mirage rising slowly out of the horizon you see the shadow-like outline of the famous Cathedral of Chartres. We spent a couple of days in and around the Cathedral. Magnificent as it is, it does not affect me as deeply as does Notre Dame de Paris—perhaps because it has no emotional connection with my life; perhaps because I see Chartres as a cathedral with some people living

34

around it while Notre Dame is so intimately bound up with the history of Paris through the centuries—its ages of splendor and glory, its dark days of subjugation and despair.

After an overnight stay in the small town of Nevers, we set out again, bound for the Riviera. But alas! Feasting the night before on *escargots de Bourgogne*, casserole-baked onion soup, yards of crusty bread and the delicious local wine had made me terribly thirsty and I drank a lot of water that night from the faucet in our room . . . something not even the greenest tourist should do in towns off the beaten track.

Retribution was swift and devastating. By the time we got to Vichy, I was feverish, aching all over and craving nothing so much as a bed and a doctor. Impossible to find a place to park, I drove around in circles until my worried wife and daughters managed to find a hotel which could accommodate us. Within minutes I was put to bed in a luxurious room with service par excellence, and with the leading physician of the town at my bedside.

His patriotic feelings hurt by my statement that it was the drinking water which had done me in, he insisted that "Monsieur le docteur just ate too much French bread. Bismuth, Madame, bismuth and charcoal tablets," he said, "will take care of it." As soon as the pharmacy reopened after the long luncheon break these were procured and did their job so well that we shall never again travel without a supply. By the time the doctor called in the next day, I was feeling fine but he instructed me to avoid drinking the Vichy water for a few days.

My indisposition gave us the opportunity to stay at one of the few hotels in the world boasting the name "Carlton" which deserves an international reputation for good taste and service. (It was the headquarters, incidentally, for Marshall Petain during the tragic life of the Vichy regime.) So here I am, sitting on the balcony, looking down at the milling crowd below.

Vichy, as you know, is a famous spa, visited by Frenchmen from all parts of France and popular with the British who like to combine a vacation with its renowned water cure. Hundreds of elegant ladies and gentlemen, as well as priests in their long robes, nuns wearing odd-shaped headgear designating their orders, and in fact people from all walks of life gather around the several sunken circles where the natural springs are located. They hand their glasses to the pretty young attendants who fill each one with the exact amount of the healing water prescribed for each individual. Sipping as they go, they promenade slowly the distance prescribed for them while the band plays overtures by Weber and Offenbach, waltzes by Strauss and all the familiar tunes which bands play all over the world.

Others rest on the many benches provided, or browse along the row of antique and jewelry shops. The walks winding endlessly through the beautiful park with its magnificent trees and flower-beds are completely covered, so that people taking the cure are always protected against rain or too much sun. It is a strange world where people are preoccupied with the hundreds of ills and pains human beings suffer with almost complete exclusion of the rest of the world.

Watching the crowd from my balcony is like sitting in the loge of a theatre. Below me is the stage, with the milling crowd enacting their particular roles in the continuous show that is our life. There is an old couple, with their water glasses in lovely containers, walking slowly arm in arm, carrying the weight of many decades on their stooped shoulders. What kind of life have they had? How much pleasure, how much pain? There, a group of children play joyfully with their colorful balls, running, jumping, falling, pushing, crowding the old ones, soon to take over the center of the stage. The curtain is the beginning for some. For others? Well, just curtain.

So the play goes on and on, without end. Once in a while one of the players stops the play and tries to explain to the generations of participants and onlookers what it is all about. A scientist, a playwright, a poet, an artist, a philosopher, an Einstein, Sophocles, Galileo, Socrates, Michelangelo, Dostoyevsky, Freud or Shakespeare. Their views, their interests and explanations, the audience they attract are as varied as the players, the scenes and the plots on the everchanging stage. Those who are not forgotten after a moment of dazzling appearance, who live on through the ages, have one thing in common: they give us some understanding about ourselves.

36

They help us to bridge the pit between those who play the lead, the support, a chorus girl or just a stage hand and the audience, regardless of whether they are sitting in the most expensive loge, the family circle, or high up in the balcony.

XII. ALL IS WELL THAT ENDS WELL

Your letter with its provocative questions about man's hostility toward woman has just arrived. I promise to answer it, but not today. We are leaving Vichy tomorrow morning and heading south toward the Riviera. We plan to follow the coastline of the Côte d/Azur, then drive through Northern Italy and South-Tyrol to Austria. If our tentative schedule holds, we should arrive in Vienna in about two weeks. Until then, I cannot be reached.

Unless we change our minds, we plan to stop for a day or so in Merano, a charming little Italian town with many hotels and sanatoriums, a favorite resort for people suffering from tuberculosis. Just as in Vichy, the guests take their daily promenades, listening to the same kind of music and carrying also little containers—they are trying to hide. There are no drinking glasses in the containers, but little jars, there are no fountains . . . and the guests are so much younger!

Three incidents come to mind when I recall the early days in Merano. Each happily illustrates the motto of the optimist that "all's well that ends well."

In 1931, a few weeks after I joined the staff of a hospital there caring for several hundred young men and women from all over the world suffering from tuberculosis, I became quite ill and ran a temperature for a few days. After a cursory examination, the chief of staff, with thirty years of experience behind him, said: "Oh, well, doctor, we all get it sooner or later. You must have noticed that two of our former staff physicians are among your patients. Treatment for employees is free as long as they need it." He never forgave me for his wrong diagnosis and revenged himself by beating me at chess every day during the entire year of my stay.

The second incident occurred while I was spending one of my rare free days skiing in the magnificent mountains surrounding Merano. A group of South Tyrolean patriots mistook me, in my dark blue shirt, for one of Mussolini's hated "Black-shirts." With unmistakable glee at having caught one of them alone, they took off after me. Either they were not as good skiers as they should have been or fright made me a better one than I was. After a terrifying race, I spotted a group of people near a small hut and headed toward them. That ended the chase.

The third episode was less dangerous than the first two and ended on a delightful note. I became friendly with a young Dutchman who was just visiting Merano as a tourist. He invited me to play bridge one afternoon, in one of the more exclusive clubs. Without the faintest notion of how high the stakes were and without sense enough to ask, we played for about three hours with a wealthy businessman from Belgium and another man who happened to be a professional member of the club. I ended up a winner and, after deducting a horren-dous amount for card fee and for glasses of Cinzano, a digni-fied, middle-aged lady handed me 4,000 lire.

I left the place in a daze, pursued by the horrifying thought, "Suppose I had lost!" You see, my pay at the hospital, exclusive of room and board, amounted to exactly 300 lire a month. After recovering from the shock, I ordered a suit from the best tailor in town and, needless to say, never went near a bridge club in Merano again. Nor did anyone in the hospital ever find out where I had spent that afternoon.

Chamonix

XIII. THE GLACIERS OF MONT BLANC

Well, here we are in Chamonix, gateway to the incomparable Mont Blanc. We never did get to the Riviera. The weather turned very warm and after an overnight stay in Lyons, we decided to go east. So instead of basking in the sunshine of southern beaches and watching the parade of bikinis, we are high up in the mountains surrounded by people sporting woolen clothing, heavy boots, neatly packed knapsacks and mountain-climbing equipment.

Interest in weather reports and exploring the glaciers replaces interest in bathing, boating, casinos and night clubs. Suntans are just as prevalent but they have a more rugged cast. There are sharp white lines around the eyes, and the tan ends abruptly in the middle of the forehead, due to the heavy sunglasses and woolen caps worn while on the glaciers.

Even though I was born on the eastern edge of the Great Hungarian Plain (the puszta), mountains have always fascinated me. They are a world unto themselves and the people who come to see them seem to undergo a change of their personality. Facing constant danger, they become more friendly, more ready to help one another. Recognizing how dependent they are on one another makes them somehow more somber, more accessible.

We arrived here during a heavy rainstorm. The tourist season is in full swing and the city is full of skiers, mountain-climbers and sightseers. It took some time to find accommodations but we did, finally, right next to the railroad station. The city seemed deserted during the heavy downpour. The moment the sun came through, hundreds of people in colorful sweaters rushed in to find seats on the first train bound for the sea of glaciers, to ski or climb, hike and visit the glacial coves which, lit by the sun as it breaks through the deep ice, look like the fairyland of one's dreams.

And here we are, seated on a beautiful terrace, sipping hot drinks and watching this fabulous world of snow and ice, of rugged mountains and endless glaciers looking like frozen turbulent rivers. Now and again, part of a snow mountain just breaks away, pouring tons of ice and snow onto a glacier. From a distance, the effect is of innocent white dust but it might just be one of those dreaded avalanches, the cold tomb of daring mountain-climbers. Far off, like a line of dots, we can see a party of climbers, securely tied with ropes, carefully skirting the gaping crevices in the glittering ice. They are led by the legendary guides of Chamonix.

The weather, the view, change constantly. Brilliant sunshine one minute—only to disappear completely in the shifting clouds with their sudden snow flurries.

Just now the rain is pouring without let up. But it is a town where people are used to it and are equipped for all possibilities. We will also put on our newly acquired waterproof hiking boots and rain gear and go out for a walk and for dinner. If the rain does not let up tonight, I may skip the cinema and answer your questions about man's hostility to women. Incidentally, your surprise that analysts also have nightmares is typical of the widespread misconceptions people have about psychoanalysts. I will go into this some other time. Meanwhile, let me assure you that psychoanalysts are just as imperfectly human as all others and that it would be most unfortunate for their patients if this were not so.

Bern

XIV. VACATION WITHOUT PLAN

Since my working life is governed by fixed daily schedules, it is one of the joys of a vacation just to be free of them. Being on a tour like this one, not bound even by plane or train schedules, is delightful. This goes for travel plans as well as for good intentions about writing letters. Specifically, the hot spiced wine we drank with dinner in Chamonix was so potent and mellowing that my mood was totally unsuited for "hostility to women."

After a long, peaceful night of sleep, I was awakened by the brilliant sunshine flooding in through our windows. In no time at all we were on our way to the cable car station, where already a long line of tourists waited eagerly for the trip to the Aiguille du Midi, about 15,000 feet up. Clouds hovered over the upper part of the ascent, so that the cars, each carrying 30 to 40 passengers, seemed to disappear into space, going straight to heaven. Finally, came a break in the clouds and before us was the breathtaking, sunlit summit of Mont Blanc. I will say no more or we'll never catch up with the days that have passed since we looked our last on the great sweep of the mountains and the toy-like houses of Chamonix as the cablecar descended a few hours later.

On our way to Bern, we had stopped to visit some dear old friends and now, sitting on the balcony of the Hotel Bellevue, we marvel another overwhelming view. This time it is the Jungfrau chain, its majestic peaks covered with fresh snow, glowing in the reddish light of the setting sun against a darkening purple sky. We plan to spend a few days in this luxurious hotel. It is time to rest from the overpowering impressions of the last few days and to prepare for all that is to come.

What a pity so many people are incapable of enjoying their

vacations! Even though they are not aware of it the pursuit of pleasure makes them feel guilty, so everything they do becomes a chore. They do not hike, swim, play tennis or take a sun bath just because they enjoy it but because "it is good for you." Golf tires them, not because of the walking involved but because their fierce competitiveness exhausts them. If they are in the mountains, they wish to be at the beach. Wherever they are, they complain about the food, the beds, the other guests, the atmosphere of the place. They do not realize that the trouble is within themselves. Yet rest, play, relaxation are absolute necessities for effective, satisfactory living.

XV. LEUKERBAD AND THE STAR OF VALAIS

We couldn't possibly come to Switzerland without dropping in on some good friends, even if it's just for an hour over a glass of wine or a cup of coffee. Our first stop was in Leukerbad, a small town high up in the mountains of the Canton Valais. It's repetitious to say "high in the mountains," but then there are only two choices in Switzerland: you are either in a valley or up in the mountains, or on the way from one to the other. The valleys are generally reserved for the larger cities.

In any case, our visit to Max Tobler and his family lasted rather longer than an hour. Max, brother of a dear friend in Los Angeles, is a fabulous host and his wife, Pola, as well as his daughters, Marianne and Barbara, have the gift of making you feel at home instantly. Only Max and Barbara were at home when we telephoned to announce our presence in the area; Pola and Marianne were en route from Zurich, their winter home. However, by the time we arrived, after two hours of driving up the steep, winding road, all four were waiting for us at the entrance to their beautiful chalet on the outskirts of the town, making us welcome with inimitable charm and warmth.

Of course they would not hear of our leaving too soon. By the time we had eaten all the meats, vegetables, cheeses, preserves, and had sampled all the famous Valais wines Max brought up from his wine cellar, we were neither in a mood nor a condition to leave. Our daughters were made comfortable

42

in an upstairs bedroom, disappearing under the fluffy feather-beds so perfect for cold mountain nights. Marianne and I were put up at a nearby hotel. Only the persuasive Toblers could have succeeded in getting us a room in the overcrowded little town.

Before we retired to our hotel, we settled down for another wine-drinking session together. They have a charming excuse in this region of Switzerland for opening the "next" bottle, if any excuse is needed: a good Valais wine, poured from a certain height by an expert hand, is supposed to form bubbles in the shape of a star—the star of Valais—on the top of the glass. The ceremony must be repeated several times before you are convinced, but by the time you are on the third bottle, you are quite ready to challenge any unbeliever to a new round of proof. As a matter of fact, I didn't stop seeing those stars of Valais even in my dreams long after we retired.

We spent the next day and night with the Toblers—eating, drinking, dancing, hiking; reminiscing about our first meeting in Zurich and their visit to Los Angeles; talking about old problems and new ones; problems of Switzerland, of Europe, of the world. By the time we were ready to leave, we felt as though we had grown up together. We could almost have been persuaded to build a chalet and settle in Leukerbad, if only land were not so terribly expensive in Switzerland.

XVI. THE MARKET

I love to go on early morning walks especially whenever I am in a strange place. I have walked in Venice at early dawn, crossing countless little bridges and narrow streets without seeing a soul except for a lone gondolier still half asleep, cleaning, caressing, getting his beloved gondola ready for the day. I have had long discussions with friendly policemen in London parks; seen fish jumping from the mirror-like fiord in Ulvik; witnessed the unloading of carloads of vegetables and the setting up of fragrant flower stalls in the harbor-market of Bergen; watched the baker boys on their bicycles delivering the first freshly baked breads and croissants to Paris cafes; and exchanged greetings with the street cleaners who, with brooms and rolled rags expertly direct the water on flooded streets to wash away a day's accumulated dirt; a couple of priests going to the early mass in Rome.

I delight to hear the sounds of early morning—the opening of windows, the clang of the first streetcars, the clatter of milk wagons, the rumble of beer barrels rolling from their trucks to the entrance of a Gasthaus, the rolling up of metal shutters as shops come to life. Now the streets are filling up—children on their way to school, office girls applying makeup on the run, more and more people, some walking leisurely, some in a great hurry. Janitors stand yawning in doorways, looking at the sky: no point in sweeping sidewalks if it is going to rain! A city awakens—a place to work, to seek pleasure or endure pain—and I am just one among thousands, no longer a stranger but part of it all.

This morning, after walking through empty arcades on the main streets of Bern, I ended up in the crowd of the early morning market. Hundreds of stalls lining both sides of street after street offer everything from food to beautiful cowbells. It seemed as if all the housewives of Bern were there, filling their baskets from the great variety of fruits and vegetables produced by the rich soil of the Berner Oberland.

Some look critically at the irregular chunks of butter ranging in color from white to deep yellow, wondering aloud whether it was freshly churned or whether *der tückishe Bauer* (tricky farmer) mixed it with an older batch. Others make disparaging remarks about the size of the eggs, and, with expert fingers, feel the breasts of screeching chickens—their feet tied, wings flapping, heads turned grotesquely upward. Still others put stalks of pink rhubarb in their bag, snapping string beans to test their tenderness, walk the rows of cheese stalls, the butcher shops and pausing before the bright flowers so neatly arranged and so fresh in their blue-enameled buckets filled with water.

And the baskets of fruit! Freshly picked cherries hanging from large branches. Berries—all kind of berries: gooseberries, currants, raspberries and to top them all, the heavenly-fragrant wild strawberries. Have you ever eaten wild strawberries? We

44

have picked them, on occasion, even in California, and on the wooded hills of Oregon. They are too delectable for words.

The shopping goes on and on—experienced, thrifty house-wives weighing the price of everything, counting their change carefully before snapping shut their large coin purses.

It is all so familiar! I close my eyes and the clock turns back half a century. How we loved to go to market! One was held every day in my home town but the Wednesday market was the largest—filling the main square and spilling over into dozens of adjacent streets.

There were no automobiles or trucks then, just horse-drawn carriages loaded with food, clothing, machinery and every-thing else imaginable—the smell of flowers mixing with the sharp odor of rows and rows of high boots made from freshly-tanned leather. There were peasants and craftsmen—experts at sharpening knives and scissors, carvers of wooden spoons, glass cutters, rows of men with sawhorses to cut logs for firewood, chimneysweeps with black faces and dozens of other artisans long since vanished. Gypsies played heart-breaking tunes, dancing in wild ecstasy and showing off their card tricks.

Occasionally, little men from a strange land on the other side of the world, communicating only with sign language, attracted crowds of open-mouthed children: enterprising Japanese selling elaborate stone carvings or simple little stone monkeys, colorful hand-painted fans and umbrellas. There were the candystalls, the toys. It was just paradise. How can children today grow up without it!

The tricks we used to play! Do you know how to buy a watermelon without paying for it? Very simple. All you need is a long string with a nail tied to one end and a bunch of adventurous kids. A group of us would join the crowds of shoppers around a room-high pyramid of watermelons. One boy would sink the nail into a melon on the ground. While some of us engaged the farmer in conversation, the rest would surround and escort away the slowly-moving melon, pulled by a conspirator at the other end of the long string. We were not always successful and scattering in predetermined directions require quick getaways, but most of the time the trick worked.

In this undertaking I participated just for the fun of it and to be a good sport, watermelon was not one of my favorite fruits.

There was another trick I thoroughly enjoyed. It required a minor cash investment. We would buy small round loaves of bread, cut them in half and eat the soft insides still warm from the oven, leaving only the thick brown crusts. Then we would walk to a dairy stall, ask for half a liter of sour cream and let the good-natured peasant woman pour it into our empty bread shells. After waiting a minute or two, we would either remark that it wasn't as fresh as we expected or admit with great embarrassment that we had no money. We would then pour the cream back into the pail and before the woman had recovered from her shock and realized our treachery, we would disappear into the maze of stalls and horse-carts and feast on our breadcrusts soaked with delicious sour cream.

Fortunately, neither we nor anyone else considered our childish pranks a form of juvenile delinqency or I might not have been permitted to enter the United States. It is a pity so many harmless pranks are labeled "juvenile delinquency" these days while more serious actions of adults are ignored or minimized. Drunken driving, for example, is considered a misdemeanor in most states while swiping a hubcap by a teenager is a felony. Of course there are many youngsters who really are delinquents, creating serious problems in every part of the world. But there are many others whose "anti-social" behavior is merely an expression of normal development—the need of adolescents to rebel against the restrictions of childhood and to assert their independence.

Some, like the neglected children of the rich or poor, beg for attention from the world of adults even if the attention takes the form of punishment. Some are sick, have no ability to judge or to conform to the requirements of reality. Many identify with the attitudes and behavior of their elders, practicing in clumsy adolescent fashion their future roles as businessmen, politicians or professionals. Unfortunately, we lump them all together, label them delinquents and treat them accordingly, often forcing them into becoming delinquents by our attitudes. Instead of understanding them, we punish them, mistaking punishment and ostracism for discipline.

A sudden argument in "Switzer" Deutch, a language impossible for me to understand, brought me back to Bern from my reveries. After buying a basket of wild strawberries and several bouquets of flowers, I returned to the hotel to join my family for breakfast.

XVII. "GROSSIE OF BERN" AND "JEANNE OF THE MOUNTAIN"

We have just returned from visiting two delightful ladies, each more than eighty years old, the mothers of friends from Bern who now live in Los Angeles. We met them first about ten years ago when we visited here at the same time as their American children, and have visited them several times since.

They are known to their families and friends as Grossie and Jeanne. It would be more accurate to call them "Grossie of the city" and "Jeanne of the mountains." They are good friends, share a common cultural background and are intelligent, alert, very much alive. They love and are loved by a large group of the same people, relatives and friends alike, yet it would be difficult to find two women so different from each other. Descriptive words like old, lovable, charming have quite different meanings when applied to Grossie and Jeanne.

Grossie is petite, fragile, a touch of pink accenting her pale cheeks. One might even suspect a wisp of makeup, a conscious bit of coquetry suggesting the faintly-blushing seductiveness of a Victorian maiden. In a quiet, unassuming way, she both expects and receives a great deal of attention. Everyone worries about her and takes care of her. She is automatically given the most comfortable chair at the head of the table. There is always someone to arrange the shawl about her shoulders, to feel guilty at having forgotten a soft pillow to support her gently-bent back. All this time, there is a youthful, impish glow in her eyes, permitting a glimpse of her sense of humor and inner strength.

For the life of me I cannot visualize her in youth as one of

47

these sturdy Swiss girls in their spiked shoes climbing the steep trails of the mountains. I see her rather as "Heidi" who never made it up to the "summer alm" in the high meadows—a slender girl with long blonde hair who would carefully arrange her starched white dress before sitting down on a clean blanket spread out for her under a shady tree, after an exhausting carriage-ride to a birthday party on the outskirts of town.

Grossie had invited us to come for *Jause* (afternoon coffee) which seemed quite natural; it wouldn't be proper, somehow, to visit her in the morning. It was a joy to see her in her charming little apartment so expressive of her personality; to share her pleasure in our reunion and the flowers we brought her. She served coffee, excellent cookies, the wonderful Swiss chocolate she always sends us at Christmas—all on exquisite china—along with raspberry syrup and soda or sherry, as one chose. We talked of many things but mainly about her children and the grandchildren in Los Angeles. Every once in a while, she would turn affectionately to our children and, with a tender touch of their cheeks, try to bridge the thousands of miles to those she loves in California.

The next day we visited Jeanne. There is no time of day when one cannot call on her—it would be perfectly all right to show up for an early breakfast. Jeanne of the mountains is a complete contrast to Grossie of Bern. One embraces Grossie to protect her, Jeanne to lean on. She is solid and strong. Her heavy mountain shoes carry a determined person who knows exactly where she is going. Her suntanned face, strong nose, thin lips, even her wrinkles are chiseled out of solid oak. She is like her chalet on the high meadow, a structure of beautiful wood standing on solid rock, aged by summer sun and winter storm. A giant apple tree covered with blossoms frames the entrance. It is a beautiful place, its long balcony overlooking a lovely garden of fruit trees, flowers, climbing vines—and beyond, the sweep of the Thuner See and the Berner Alpen.

It was many years ago that she and her husband left Bern and built the chalet. She told us about the difficulties they had faced at first. They were strangers to those who had lived in these mountains for centuries and these mountaineers do not

Shopping on Montmartre

Painter on Montmartre

M. Porisse with his little girl

Narrow street leading to the Cathedral in Chartres

In Obergrindelwald, Switzerland

Watching the mountain climbers

Mont Blanc — going straight up to Heaven

The glaciers of Mont Blanc — look like
frozen turbulent rivers

Near the top of the Jungfrau

Wading in a rushing mountain creek in Tyrol

Drying hay in Vorarlberg

Spring in Switzerland

easily trust or even speak to strangers, especially to those from the big city with the title of "Doctor." Then one day, just when the freshly cut grass was drying into valuable hay, a sudden thunderstorm threatened the entire crop. Everyone within reach who could lift a fork, men, women and children pitched in to gather as much of the crop as possible.

Jeanne and her husband were among them with their pitchforks, bracing themselves against the wind, not letting up until the work was done, until, exhausted, all were driven to take cover from the drenching rain and pelting hail. From that day forward, they were accepted as respected members of the far-flung community. There is no one in those hills now who would not answer her yodel-like call or who does not know that her help is there if needed.

Jeanne is a longtime widow and lives alone, but she would not think of leaving her chalet. She has zest, curiosity, loves life and everything that lives. She tells wonderful stories about the mountains she knows so well. By the time you finish the second cup of absinthe she has prepared, you are ready to spread your wings and join the birds circling lazily overhead.

Time spent with Grossie and Jeanne makes one wonder why there is so much emphasis on youth, especially in the United States. Why should one be so afraid of growing old? Certainly Jeanne complains too. Not because she is frightened or feels worthless but because she can no longer do all the things she used to do, like hiking for hours over the beautiful trails leading from her chalet, to discover a new plant, a new flower, a little bird needing help—simple joys which in our own country are denied to young and old alike, since we have been blessed with automobiles and superhighways.

Despite their differences, Grossie and Jeanne have this in common: both have been widows for many years, living their own lives in a city apartment or a mountain chalet. They are alone, yes, but they are not withdrawn nor excluded from the world around them. They are a part of their community, young and old, sharing in the interests, advantages, limitations and handicaps every age of life entails.

Old people belong just as much in the total picture as

children do—and in the interest of both. It is as grave a mistake to build special communities for "senior citizens" as it would be to isolate children in separate communities. One is as unnatural as the other. Children could not grow up successfully under these conditions and old people lose their sense of belonging, their purpose in life, with nothing to look forward to but infirmity and death. . . .

It was difficult to bid farewell to our old friends—Grossie, misty-eyed, in the doorway of her apartment and Jeanne on her balcony, standing straight and tall in harmony with her timeless surroundings.

Grindelwald

XVIII. GAMBLING AND MOUNTAIN CLIMBING

We have been in Grindelwald for the last few days. The weather is superb, the deep blue sky contrasting vividly with the snow-capped peaks of the Jungfrau. Marianne, who is good at it, has found us a very comfortable small pension on the edge of town. From our balcony, all we can see are the majestic mountains and the flowering meadows. The only sound is the tinkle of the cowbells, loud enough to wake us early in the morning, then fading as the cows climb higher and higher to graze. At sundown, they return, picking their way carefully down the steep slopes.

For two days now, the repeated, ominous ringing of church bells has punctuated the tense atmosphere of this little town. Young men from many countries are ascending the dangerous Northwall, as hundreds of local people and tourists stand vigil day and night. Some have powerful binoculars. Others try, hands cupped over eyes, to make out the figures of the struggling climbers as they inch their way up the forbidding rocks.

Cheers break out at news of success; painful silence accompanies the rescue teams carrying the broken bodies of several young men to the little church. They have joined the countless others who, throughout history, have given their lives in man's irresistible urge to conquer nature. They attempt it on the sheer cliffs of the rugged giants, in chemical laboratories and medical schools, in thousands of research centers, in the capsules of rockets racing toward the moon.

You asked me once whether this urge has anything to do with gambling, with testing Lady Luck in order to force her to prove her love. Perhaps it may be traced back to some common basis in childhood: such men may be searching on a deep level for proof of the infinite, magical love of the mother who can protect against all harm—or for proof of their own magical power to overcome any danger, any obstacle. But there is a big difference between the joy of a man hoisting a flag on a mountaintop, the researcher discovering a vaccine against a ruthless killer of millions, the astronaut emerging from his capsule after circling the earth and the angry, anxious gambler shooting his dice, his pleading cry: "Come seven, come eleven, baby needs a pair of shoes," his moods alternating rapidly between elation with a "natural" and depression from "snake eyes."

No, they are not the same. They are as opposite as health and illness, as hope and despair, as achievement and failure.

Austria

XIX. THE COWARD BEHIND THE BULLY

We have covered quite a lot of ground since leaving Grindelwald and settling down in this quaint little lake resort in Austria for a few days' rest. On our way through Switzerland in the middle of August we were snowed in at Pontresina, drove through Engadin in a pouring rain and spent a couple of days in Innsbruck, where we heard a delightful concert on a centuries-old wooden organ in the tiny "Silver Chapel." It sounded like an entire wood-wind orchestra ranging from flute to bassoon, combined with a few whining, complaining tones like those of an old recorder.

We ate breakfast on the Grossglockner, the highest mountain in Austria. Following the advice of our innkeeper, we started at five in the morning to avoid the German invasion—the thousands of Germans who come to the lakes and mountains to take advantage of the low prices in Austria. They come in buses and countless Volkswagens, crowding the roads and parking places, the trains and cable-cars. Their loud voices echo through the mountains, their beer-garden singing reaches across lakes, streets, hotel corridors, on and on, late into the night. They are either unaware of or totally insensitive to the almost universal dislikes of them all over Europe. They are hated openly and intensely in Norway, Holland, Denmark— ignored, mistrusted or treated with cool politeness in other places.

My dislike and mistrust date back to my first contact with them when, during the First World War, one of the Prussian divisions was stationed in our city. Then as always they treated allies like victims, creating terror and resentment everywhere. I was too young then to know what I learned much later, that behind a big bully there is usually a coward who has to prove to himself and others that he is not afraid. However, I recall an incident which proved this point so well.

My oldest sister, Helen, attractive and capable, was a popular administrator in the German army hospital. On her birthday, about twenty officers, looking like giants to me, came to our house to give her a surprise party. They came loaded down with caviar, champagne, all manner of delicacies looted from a starving city—walking in heavy, hobnailed boots like the Pinzgauer horses pulling their heavy lorries. They decorated our dining room with colorful papers and beautiful woodcarvings made by Russian prisoners. They gave her presents of chocolate, coffee, tea and fabrics, none of which were available to the inhabitants of our city. There was feasting and drinking —toasts to the Kaiser, the "glorious" German Army, to victory.

Following an old Hungarian custom on festive occasions and during the bitterly cold winters, tea at the end of the dinner was served in an unusual and charming way. All the lights were turned off and teacups on large trays were brought in. The bluish flames of burning rum poured over sugar in each cup lit up the dark room. The German officers, obviously unfamiliar with the custom and expecting something terrible to happen, jumped to their feet.

In the deadly silence that followed, the sizzling of the melting sugar, the shadows of the flickering lights playing on the dark walls and on the pale, terrified faces of the officers, made the scene even more eerie and ominous. Only the absolute calmness of my mother prevented a dangerous panic. Before anyone could move, she poured boiling tea into her cup and raised it to her lips. The lights were turned on, she wished everyone a pleasant evening and, her glance motioning me to follow her, left the room.

XX. THE GHOSTS OF THE PAST AND THE TRAGEDY OF AUSTRIA

No matter how often we return to Austria, every visit remains the same stirring experience. We have been at many places connected with intimate personal experiences and it is difficult to write about them.

School is out. The highways and resorts are crowded. The Salzburg Festival is in full swing and the city is jammed. With great difficulty we managed to find a place to park. Unthinkable to drive through Salzburg without stopping to feast on *Salzburger-Nockerln*, a dessert served in huge quantities. It has uncountable calories and enough cholesterol to floor ten heart specialists but it's delicious and contains all the ingredients that make the Austrian women look so attractive in their colorful dirndls.

We stopped in Saalbach, for years one of my chosen ski haunts; spent a night in Hallstadt, an ancient little town looking as if it had slipped from the steep hills down to the lake. And we visited Grundlsee, once the favorite meeting ground for Marianne's family.

Wherever we go, the people are friendly, and occasionally apologetic. The majority are anxious to impress you with their dislike of the Germans, their suffering during the Nazi years and the long, horrible war. Here and there, a middle-aged man with a Hitler moustache provokes the painful thought: "Whom did you kill . . . an old man, a woman, a child, a friend, a relative or one of those hundreds of familiar faces one greets with a smile?" I reach for Marianne's hand, draw my children closer and think of those we were powerless to protect and of the millions who had no one to protect them.

How nice it would be to write only about the charm of the Austrian countryside, the beautiful lakes and forests and mountains, the endless walks, the sudden thunderstorms so frequent in Salzkammergut—but it would be forced, it wouldn't be honest and it would be wrong. You were not yet born when it all began and probably didn't learn much about it in school. Still, we must try to learn from history or we shall continue to repeat the horrible mistakes of the past.

It was here, in the small towns of the provinces that the exaggerated nationalistic movements started after the First World War and were later nourished by German Nazism on one frontier and by Italian Fascism on the other. The City Governments of Vienna (which contained almost one-third of the entire Austrian population) and of the other industrial

55

centers were controlled by the liberal Social Democrats, after 1918, but the national government, because of the preponderance of provincial representatives, was conservative, to say the least.

The rural districts mistrusted and opposed the Social Democrats. The reactionary forces in the provinces were constantly gaining strength. Small groups of illegally organized minutemen were encouraged by disillusioned officers of the defeated, disbanded army, by the big landowners and the bankrupt nobility of the dismembered Empire. Gradually, they found support, openly or secretly, in the cities. In Vienna, they became a haven for the misfits, the chronic malcontents and were joined by the victims of the terrible post-war economic conditions, particularly by the impoverished middle class which included the small merchants, the clerical workers and the displaced bureaucrats of the once far-flung Empire. These people had been left rootless in a new society. Conditioned by centuries of tradition, unable to adjust to this new world, to their lost status, they lived shabbily year after year on inadequate pensions, dreaming of the past and looking for scapegoats.

Anti-Semitism as a scapegoat is as old in Austria as its history. The new wave of Anti-Semitism, after World War I, spread rapidly from Vorarlberg and the Tyrol to the other provinces, and then to the cities including, of course, Vienna. *Der Jud und der Radfahrer* ("the Jew and the Bicycle-Rider") were made jokingly responsible for all mishaps. (This commonly-used expression in Vienna dated back to the time when bicycle-riders were as dangerous as automobile-drivers later became.)

The sign *Juden, Neger und Hunde Verboten* displayed on student restaurants was not an innovation of Hitler's, nor even of the famous anti-Semitic mayor of Vienna, Karl Lueger. "Jews, Negroes and Dogs Forbidden." Thought-provoking, isn't it? They knew dogs, of course, and certainly had encountered Jews (or as Lueger put it, "I decide who is a Jew")—but most of them had never even seen a Negro!

There were secret Nazi organizations, especially in the uni-

56

versities, as early as the 1920's. You may recall that Hitler began organizing a National Socialist Party in Austria in the middle 20's, some years before he was expelled from the country. Incidentally, I got my first beating as a Jew in 1927. However, during those years, the most hated enemy of the reactionary forces was personified by the Social Democrats who had controlled the government of Vienna without interruption since the end of the First World War. They had introduced reforms which benefitted the entire population but above all the workers, the class of citizens who were replacing the old middle class. The workers were housed in specially-built, comfortable apartments, received expanding social security benefits and government health insurance.

By contrast to Vienna where the Social Democrats were in power, the Conservative Party, supported by the representatives from the rural districts, maintained a precarious majority in the national government. The difference between the two parties was great, far greater than between the Conservatives and the Liberals in England or the Democrats and Republicans in the United States. They represented two different worlds. The Christian Socialists included all the reactionary forces, from the royalists dreaming of a return of the Habsburgs and Crown Prince Otto to the arch-conservative Catholic Church, the state religion of Austria. It was the party of the displaced middle class and small bureaucrats in the cities, the bearded Tyrolean peasants resistant to any change and the titled landowners in their castles, living as if feudalism and serfdom were still the law of the land.

The social Democrats included most of the workers in Vienna, in Graz, Klagenfurt and the other industrial centers; the postwar generation of intellectuals and professionals—writers, doctors, lawyers, engineers, teachers. The Social Democrats opposed the old caste system but jealously guarded and promoted the cultural and artistic heritage of the old Empire. Although there were fringe groups of extremists within and outside the two parties, these were, for a long time, weak and powerless.

The two parties fought each other with every means at their

disposal, including their considerable economic influence. The Social Democrats controlled employment and housing in the cities at a time when jobs were at a premium and apartments practically unattainable. This was matched by the Christian Socialists' control of government facilities and employment in the provinces and in the army.

The constant clashes between the two parties were not confined to editorials in the newspapers, debates in Parliament and marching demonstrators. Physical fighting, insignificant at first, was increasing and spreading throughout the country.

The University in Vienna, with an ancient charter guaranteeing its independence, became an ideal battleground. Students of the University were also its citizens, granted special privileges. Even though it came under the jurisdiction of the Ministry of Education, no policeman was permitted to enter its grounds or to arrest a student, unless requested to do so by the University authorities. Many bloody fights took place on its very steps, while police stood by with patrol wagons and ambulances, powerless to interfere so long as the participants remained on the privileged university grounds.

Even though most of the students were not card-carrying members of either party, they were emotionally drawn to one or the other and the battles—joined by the thousands of foreign students—were fierce. The most clear-cut divisions existed among the medical students working in the Institute of Anatomy, situated a few blocks from the main building. The building housed two separate departments of anatomy of equal official standing. Students were free to choose which to attend.

Professor Julius Tandler was the chairman of the department of functional anatomy. He was a brilliant thinker, an outstanding lecturer and teacher and a hard taskmaster, with a notable sense of humor. He was also one of the leaders of the Social Democrats and a member of the City Council of Vienna. He was the choice of the liberals and of practically all the foreign students with the exception of the Germans. He was also favored by the Jews, by most of the women students and even by some politically conservative students who nevertheless wanted to benefit from his unusual ability.

58

The chairman of the other department was a dull, colorless, scientifically insignificant old man who taught descriptive anatomy in the most unimaginative fashion. Without exception, members of all the reactionary, anti-Semitic, beer-drinking and duelling fraternities were his students.

In spite of the fact that he rarely flunked anyone while Tandler flunked students by the dozen, resulting in a year or two of lost time, Tandler's students outnumbered the other professor's two to one. But you wouldn't have thought so when fighting broke out.

The Nationalists were a small but well-organized militant minority who planned their battles systematically—sometimes against the political opposition; sometimes in an attempt to "get that Red, Tandler!" and sometimes just for the fun of it. They used clubs, hose, blackjacks—all the paraphernalia suitable for close fighting. The rest of us were untrained, unwilling contenders, always on the defensive. We used fists, books and human bones hastily borrowed from the dissecting rooms. If things got too rough, we were joined by the janitors and younger professors, using our most effective weapon, the water-hose.

Practically no communication existed between the two anatomy classes, either on the faculty or the student level, except that on rare occasions a member of the opposing group would relent enough to warn us: "Don't come to the Institute tomorrow, we're planning to beat you up!" Slowly, reluctantly, nursing bloody heads, we—and even more, those who came after us—had to learn that a book and a human bone are no match for a blackjack, lead pipe or hobnailed boot.

In a way, the same thing was happening throughout the entire country. A militant minority, self-appointed patriots longingly looking backwards, were increasing their activities especially in the provinces. At first, they were merely tolerated. Later, they were encouraged and utilized by powerful reactionary forces inside and outside the national government. In the late 20's, the members of this minority seemed to be a unified group but before long, differences began to show up, preparing the ground for dangerous conflicts to come. The

59

right-wing coalition consisted of the Nazi and the royalists; halfway between them, ideologically, were the Christian Socialists. The latter formed the government but only with the support of the Nazis and the royalists were they able to maintain a precarious lead over the Social Democrats. Fear and opposition to the Social Democrats—"Die Verfluchten Sozies" (the accursed Sozies)—was the issue which held them together. When forces unite *against* something and not *for* something, their destruction seems to be inevitable.

Encouraged by the success of Hitler and his Nazis in Germany, the Nazi Party in Austria adopted the same techniques of intimidation and grew by leaps and bounds. Using the methods of Hitler's Storm Troopers increasingly violent clashes erupted between the Nazis and the other segments of the right-wing coalition. Fists, sticks and stones were replaced by knives, guns and hand grenades.

The Social Democrats, threatened by all the right-wing forces, reacted by tightening their own organizations in order to defend themselves and to safeguard the new way of life. Regardless of their political differences, however, the Christian Socialists, the Social Democrats and the royalists were as one in their devotion to their native historical, cultural and artistic heritage and to the perpetuation of an independent, sovereign Austria.

It didn't make any difference whether their devotion was to Beethoven, Mozart or Johann Strauss; to their celebrated Opera or to the popular music of their parks and wine cellars; to the lakes of Salzkammergut or to the Blue Danube; to the Wienerwald surrounding Vienna or to the glaciers of the Austrian Alps. They loved their horse-carriages, their theatres, the Salzburg Festivals, the heated political debates in the coffee-houses and the unforgettable organ concerts in St. Stephen's Church.

It was only the Nazi Party which demanded the abolition of Austria as a separate entity. They connived and plotted to dissolve it into the German Reich, making it disappear like a lump of snow or a pinch of salt in a bucket of water.

The strength of the Nazis in the Parliament had increased so greatly that shortly after Hitler's takeover in Germany they requested *Anschluss*. Their motion for Austria to become part of the Greater Germany failed by one vote only. Now supported and armed by Germany, their violence increased daily, threatening chaotic civil war.

Engelbert Dollfuss, Chancellor of Austria and leader of the Christian Socialists turned the power of the Government against them and the Nazi Party was officially outlawed. However, this did not end their machinations. As later events proved, they infiltrated every branch of the Government, especially the army and the law enforcement agencies, and thus were able to take over the country four years later in a matter of hours, without a shot being fired.

In the interim, however, the Government, headed by Dollfuss, was foolish enough to believe that it had dealt successfully with the Nazis and that it could resume its struggle with the Social Democrats. Encouraged by the ghosts of the Old Empire emerging from their medieval castles, from obscurity and retirement, it refused to recognize that it was a minority party and that unless it made peace with the Social Democrats, it could not possibly survive.

There were the marching Hahnenschwanzler (the most powerful paramilitary organization) in their ill-fitting green uniforms and green hats sporting long black cock-feathers. They looked so ridiculous that people stood on the Ringstrasse and laughed at them. But their numbers grew, their leaders became bolder, more demanding. Germany had its Brown Shirts, Italy its Black Shirts—why not Green Shirts in Austria?

There was little Chancellor Dollfuss, encouraged by his friends and advisers, indulging in unrealistic dreams. If there could be a Third Reich, why not a Third Austria? If Mussolini could become *Il Duce*, a little Austrian corporal *Der Führer* of the "Master Race," why could not I, Dollfuss (who had become an army officer by special dispensation even though he was less than five feet tall) become Father of My Country? After all, I don't want to be a Kaiser, I don't want to conquer

61

territories, I just want to be a little brother to Hitler and Mussolini . . . a benevolent Little Father who knows what is best for Austria.

And there were the ghosts of the old Empire urging him on, promising support: "Now that the bad Nazis have been dealt with, it would all be so simple if only the *Verfluchten Sozies* didn't stand in the way. Get rid of them, we'll help you," the voices from the past said. "It will make everything so easy. We will have only one party, like our great neighbors. No more depending on a majority of one representative who might get sick just when we need him most. No questioning, no criticism, no divided powers. It is about time we stopped these dangerous social reformers. Hospitals, medical care, children's play-grounds, fancy housing for workers! Who ever heard of spend-ing the taxpayers' money for school lunches, summer vacations for poor children, swimming pools for the workers, public baths, and all the other things these Reds think up every day just to make people loafers. Kaiser Franz Josef would turn in his grave! We'll have a big army with lots of officers. They will all have warm uniforms and heavy boots and real guns. And there will be parades, lots of parades like in the old days . . . if only the accursed Sozies . . ."

And so it went. Instead of cooperating, the opposing forces became more and more irreconcilable so that a head-on clash became inevitable. The Government, afraid of the Social Democrats, prodded by the reactionary forces it had to rely on for functioning and with which it was in full sympathy ideo-logically, decided that the time had come to break the power of the hated Social Democrats. Whether they actually believed it or not, the Government insisted that the Social Democrats were planning to revolt. It ordered them to disarm and when they refused, it launched a coordinated, full-scale attack.

The Civil War was on. On a cold morning in February 1934, there were barricades on the streets and once again I heard the sound of artillery. Suddenly there were troops of soldiers everywhere. The black-feathered hats of the *Hahnenschwanzler* had been replaced by steel helmets. Their leaders, some with names unheard since the collapse of the Empire in 1918, egged

62

them on. Eyes gleaming with triumph, they looked straight back to old glories, power, prestige, receptions at the Royal Palace, perhaps even a Kaiser for a symbol.

They caught the Social Democrats by surprise. Most of their leaders were arrested during the first few hours. Others barricaded themselves in the beautiful workers' apartments they were so proud of. They refused to give up, they fought back. Artillery was brought up and began to shell these "fortifications." In its misguided blindness, the Government did not realize that the first gaping holes torn into these walls marked the beginning of the destruction that would overtake Austria a few years later.

There were about two hundred women in our hospital, many with newborn babies, others recuperating from surgery. None were prepared for what was happening. Is it possible that the husbands, sweethearts, sons and daughters who had visited them the night before would not have talked about it if they were really "plotting" to take over the Government by force? Now, only a few hours later, they were fighting, bleeding, torn to bits by shells and hand grenades in their cherished apartments where empty cribs waited for new babies to come home. Now the cribs were splintered, the pretty layettes provided by the City covered with blood.

Looking back now, more than thirty-five years later, it is fair to say that I did not know a single individual personally who even dreamed it could happen in spite of my wide acquaintance among the patients, employees, doctors, nurses. None of my friends among the artists, business and professional men expected it. Either it was an extremely well-kept secret among those high up or I was more naive and ignorant than I would like to believe.

For three days and three nights the fighting raged, in Vienna, in Graz, in Klagenfurt, in the provinces. Then it was over. A few leaders of the "revolution" escaped. Some were carried on litters to the gallows, many to jails. How convenient that the death penalty, which has been abolished after the First World War, had again become the law of the land!

The leaders of the Government, convinced of their righteousness, recorded the first victory of the Austrian Army since the turn of the century! Against their own most loyal citizens! Thus they destroyed the only force which might have postponed, perhaps even prevented the inevitable doom.

These events established a perfect timetable for Hitler. He could have taken Austria by force at any time, and would have done so if necessary. But unquestionably, he preferred it this way. Now he could wait, prepare for the hour when he, who had been banished from his native land, would return to Austria not as an enemy, a conqueror at the head of his victorious armies, not as the little corporal, the penniless failure, the provincial burgher with whom the noble ghosts of the past would not shake hands or sit down at a table. No, he would return as their Savior, the Fuhrer of all Germans—and the nobles would tremble at the sight of him and pay him homage.

In the meantime, Dollfuss joined the ranks of those little men of history who try in one way or another to compensate for their short stature. It is known as the megalomania of the little man—some physically small, others suffering from feelings of worthlessness. Some are driven by an insatiable lust for power and conquest, like Napoleon, or with an unquenchable thirst for revenge, like Hitler. Some, seemingly more modest, try to create and maintain untenable situations. Dollfuss belonged in the latter category. I am sure he firmly believed, as did his successor, Chancellor Kurt Schuschnigg, that they could maintain an independent Austria, autocratic in its organization—trying out for size the models of Germany and Italy but leaning more toward Mussolini as a model. Dollfuss didn't want to be an absolute dictator. He wanted jails, but not concentration camps. He didn't want to exterminate the Jews, just to make life more difficult for them, as it had been in the good old days before that dangerous notion of democracy got into people's heads.

Only megalomania could have made Dollfuss misjudge reality so greatly that he could believe in the stability of a state where those who thought as he did were always in the minority. Only he could believe that outlawing the Nazi Party had eliminated it, that destroying the strong Social Democratic

Party would further his aims, that the royalist remnants of the past would really support him.

Five months later he lay in his office bleeding to death, assassinated by a group of Nazis in Austrian Army uniforms who would not permit his helpless successor to call a doctor.

Chancellor Schuschnigg, the unimaginative, uninspiring successor of the more authoritarian, more driven Dollfuss, became the caretaker of Austria until Hitler was ready to take over officially. The leaders of the attempted Nazi *putsch* were hanged, just as some of the leaders of the hated *Sozies* had been several months before. But Schuschnigg, no more than Dollfuss, seemed to realize what changes were taking place throughout the country. These were exemplified by what was going on even in the hospital where I worked. The same nurses and janitors who had been members of the Social Democratic Party for years and who, after that fateful February, had joined the Christian Socialists would, by the time I left Austria a year later, have secretly joined the Nazi Party. Under the leadership of the chief nurse, they studied *Mein Kampf* and practiced the battle cry of the Nazi: *"Heute gehört uns Deutschland, morgen die ganze Welt."* (Today Germany belongs to us, tomorrow the whole world.)

It was ironic that four years later to the day that the clash with the Social Democrats had erupted, on February 12, 1938, Schuschnigg was summoned to Berchtesgaden by Hitler and given the terms of surrender. After an unrealistic, last-minute gesture of defiance, Austria disappeared.

It may be worthwhile to mention two statements made to me that day in Los Angeles, when over the radio came a roar of "Heil Hitler"—"Sieg Heil"—greeting the triumphant little corporal on his march through Vienna. For months I had been begging friends and relatives to get out of Austria before it was too late. The human need to deny danger, the inability to learn from the experience of others, the wishful thinking of Herr Schuschnigg combined with the lack of information available in an autocratic state, made it hopeless.

The two statements were made by two old ladies from two different parts of the world and they provide a clearer explanation of human fate than any long scientific sociological or political dissertation. One came in a letter from Vienna: "We can't understand why you are so concerned about us. You have your Roosevelt, we have our Schuschnigg to rely on. I assure you, we have much more reason to worry about you on account of the flood in Los Angeles."

A few hours later, a charming old lady from Pasadena was sitting in my office. Aware of my anxiety, knowing of my frantic attempts to get Marianne out of Austria, she said with great sympathy: "Oh, I never realized that Hitler would turn out to be such a bad man. But of course only God knows how bad Roosevelt will turn out to be!"

Vienna

XXI. HATE, PREJUDICE AND VIOLENCE

We arrived in Vienna late last night after a long and arduous drive. The heat is unbearable and after weeks of hiking in quiet forests, the noise of the city is quite troublesome but we'll get used to it.

Many things have changed since I left here in 1935. Many more since Marianne left three years later. Through the generous help of a complete stranger, she had succeeded in getting out of Vienna six weeks after Hitler took over Austria. It took a year before she could talk about the horrors of those weeks or stop waking up in terror from torturing nightmares. And that was just the beginning!

Her sister managed to leave a few months later. Her mother was one of the few persons who did not use her American visa to leave as soon as she might have. With a large family there, including her 90-year-old mother, and with a score of friends living with her after they had been driven out of their homes by the Nazis, she postponed leaving until some of them succeeded in getting out. But her mother, her brothers with their families, and most of her friends ended up in concentration camps. Finally, at just about the last minute before it would have been too late, she managed to get away.

In 1956, after years of hesitation, we came back to Austria for our first visit. A favorite uncle of Marianne's and his daughter were the only survivors of her family still living in Vienna. The story of their life during those years would make terrible reading. There was also Emmy, a tiny old woman who had been Marianne's nurse since babyhood. Within a few minutes of our arrival, we were reunited. Were it not for their presence, I doubt that we could have forced ourselves to return. For years, the very thought of it horrified me and I was

67

haunted by a fantasy—shared by some of my friends of similar background—that if I ever went back, I would die.

Anyone who understands the meaning of ambivalence toward loved ones will recognize the guilt behind the fantasy. It manifests itself whenever someone close to us dies, especially if they die by violence. The extent of the violence of those years is so horrendous that it staggers the imagination; it is without parallel in the violence-filled history of the human race. So is the universal guilt reaction of the survivors.

We heard from eye-witnesses of the fate that had befallen our families and friends. You have read about all this in books and official records; seen countless films, witnessed the trials of war criminals on television. But can you—can anyone not intimately involved really grasp the enormity of the tragedy?

It is one thing to visualize from a distance the nameless, faceless millions who suffered and died their tortured deaths. It is quite another thing to lose close to a hundred members of your own family, innumerable friends, schoolmates, co-workers—so many, many people you have loved and admired, whose thoughts, feelings, hopes and idiosyncrasies were so much a part of you . . .

Can anyone realize, who has not lived it, the utter desolation of holding in one's hand a letter (held up for years by the British censors) from a beloved father written to his son shortly before his murder at the age of 85? "My dear son, you in the United States know better than we what will happen to us. Only America can do something about it . . . if anyone can."

And what if, in those sealed cattle-cars slowly rolling from Rumania, Hungary and Czechoslovakia with their vast burden of beaten, tortured, emaciated bodies toward Auschwitz, Buchenwald and all the other infamous place names which have replaced the honored names of Goethe, Schiller and Heine on the roster of the "Master Race"—what if among them were five of your sisters, their children and grandchildren (the husbands already worked to death in labor camps), the uncles and aunts and cousins you grew up with, the sweethearts of your youth, the playmates who were crushed against you on that crowded train in 1914, fleeing from the Russian breakthrough?

68

We asked about the lovely wire-haired terrier I had given to Marianne before leaving Vienna. You may wonder how I can talk about a dog after all what I just told you, but perhaps this story, as much as any other, points up the insanity, the depths to which man's cruelty, his pleasure in inflicting pain can carry him. I am not talking now merely of "depraved," 'degenerate," "sick" individuals—not just of an Eichmann or of the killer Himmler with his tender love of roses, but of potentially all men, particularly if pleasure in violence is exploited at an early age.

On a delightful spring evening I had taken Marianne to one of the kennels on the outskirts of Vienna. She has always loved everything alive and her pleasure in the rollicking little puppies was a joy to watch. I bought her a beautiful wire-haired terrier who became her devoted companion until she had to leave Vienna. Rick stayed with Marianne's mother until she left. What happened to him after that we could not discover but we were told what happened to the kennel, one of the best in the country for Wire-Haired Terriers, Kerry Blues and Bedlingtons.

When the Germans arrived, they learned that the kennel owners were Jewish. No one knows what happened to them (there were not many choices) but let me tell you what became of those delightful animals. The young heroes of the Master Race, descendants of Wotan, Siegfried, Brünhilde and the Valkyries and yes, of Valhalla itself, declared that *"Jüdische Hunde brauchen nicht essen."* ("Jewish dogs don't have to eat.") For days they amused themselves listening to the soul-piercing howls and watching as these magnificent animals, crazed by hunger, tore their puppies and each other to pieces ... until there was silence.

What can one do with all that? One can live in terror for the rest of one's life, full of hate, full of bitterness, full of self-destruction. Or one can devote one's life trying to understand man's need, man's pleasure in violence and to teach, judges, doctors, lawyers, to all people who are willing and those who are not willing to listen what one has learned. We can also try to promote everything that can counteract, neutralize this horrible need, try to promote culture, art, beauty; teach the ways this tremendous energy can be used constructively for life, for giving and experiencing pleasure, and not only for destruction, for inflicting pain. As I told you so many times it takes the same energy to kiss or to bite; the cattle-prodder and the flashlight use the same battery.

XXII. YES, FREUD HAS RETURNED

In May of 1956, we were in London to attend the centennial celebration of Freud's birth, a memorable affair lasting several days. There were meetings, lectures and receptions attended by the highest civic and scientific authorities of London and by psychoanalysts from the four corners of the earth. One of the most memorable events was the unveiling of a commemorative plaque on the Freud home by the city of London.

It was unusually warm and sunny for early May in England and the garden reception given by Anna Freud afterwards was delightful. We had wondered whether it would be all right to bring our young daughters, knowing how large an attendance was expected. After some hesitation I asked the Arrangements Committee. The reply I received was something we learned to appreciate later as positively an expression of British enthusiasm. It did not seem so at the time since, with my Austro-Hungarian background, I have a livelier way of expressing emotions. Anyhow, they did not say no so we took the children, to their delight.

Maresfield Gardens is a lovely street with beautiful gardens and trees. The rows of chairs in front of the Freud house, around the speakers' stand, were filled early, and a large crowd was standing outside in the street. For the dozens of children present, Anna Freud, with her deep affection and understanding for them, had made special provision. In front of the dignitaries' chairs, just under the speakers' stand, blankets had been spread on the grass and reserved for them as her special guests of honor.

It was from this glowing London experience that we had gone on to Vienna. We knew that a plaque had been placed on Freud's house in the Berggasse by the American Psychiatric

Association and we wanted to see the house again. In 1956, however, we could not find anyone who knew where it was. As a matter of fact, there was no one who knew anything about Freud even in his own house. We stood in the courtyard with its little well, then started up the neglected staircase. But the building was occupied by strangers and by workshops. The spirit of Freud had fled to the beautiful house in London with its windows overlooking the flower-filled garden ... to the city where he had been welcomed and honored, where he was able to spend the last years of his life in peace and security.

From Freud's house, we had walked to the nearby University. In the Aula, the corridors around an enclosed garden, are the busts, statues and plaques honoring the great and not-so-great people in the history of the University. Near the offices of the Medical School we found the bronze bust of Freud donated by friends from the United States after the Second World War. There were several small wreaths at the base of the pedestal. As we stood before it, a group of students gathered around trying to make out the name of the man the foreign visitors were looking at. It was obvious that they didn't recognize it, and it came as a shock to realize that they were just about learning to speak when Marie Bonaparte helped Freud to leave Vienna, when he had to promise not to return, when his books were taken from the libraries and burned and the mention of his name was prohibited.

Now at last the barbarians are gone and Freud is very much in evidence—in the Hall of Fame, in the libraries, in the minds of a new generation of students who are eager to learn all he can teach them about the human spirit in health and in sickness. This very day the International Psychotherapy Congress is meeting at the University. The Aula and the lecture halls are filled with participants. The Vienna Philharmonic has come back from Salzburg for an evening just to give a concert for us. A dinner for a thousand people took place in the ballroom of the Imperial Palace. This is not primarily a psychoanalytic conference but dozens of psychoanalysts from all over the world are participating in the discussions and giving lectures in German, French and English.

Yes, Freud has returned. One can banish, burn books, prohibit thought and speech. It has been done throughout history by tyrants, by autocratic states, by those who call ignorance their ally and fear knowledge more than the sword of their enemies. But in the long run, they can neither banish nor kill the ideas of great men.

Postscript: Dated June, 1971, the following note appeared in the *Newsletter* of the American Psychoanalytic Association. "On June 15, 1971, Sigmund Freud's apartment in Berggasse 19 was dedicated to public use as a museum, library and historic place of remembrance. The Federal Chancellor of Austria, Dr. Bruno Kreisky, and the Honorable Felix Slavik, Mayor of Vienna, officiated at the opening ceremonies, thus expressing, however belatedly, Austria's official recognition of the importance of Freud and his work.

The Sigmund Freud Gesellschaft of Vienna has carried out the acquisition and refurnishing of the Freud apartment (with the active interest and help of Miss Anna Freud) and expects to welcome the participants of the International Congress in Vienna at the Berggasse in July 1971."

XXIII. THE NEW VIENNA

Vienna is a pleasant place today. The city—apparently all of Austria—is enjoying an economic and cultural renaissance not experienced since before the First World War. Vienna, once the political, economic and cultural center of an empire, was like the big head of a giant left without a body after 1918. The empire to the east was lost. The new countries promoted their own culture in their own centers like Prague, Budapest, Bucharest, Zagreb. Vienna lost meaning to them. During the Anschluss it was further reduced to nothing more than one of the many provincial capitals of Germany.

The honeymoon with Hitler had been short-lived. He did not return as the local boy who had made good but as the paranoid, megalomanic Savior, eager to avenge the humiliation of having been banished from his native land as an obnoxious psychopath. Austria was treated like an occupied country. The Germans, with their cold, compulsive efficiency, disdained and thoroughly mistrusted the Viennese light-opera-and-chocolate-soldier military attitude. Resenting their mistreatment, the Austrians' traditional dislike of the Germans grew to hostility and finally, in the terminal months of the war, open mutiny broke out against the German Army. As a last revenge, the retreating SS troops zeroed in on Saint Stephanskirche, the famous thousand-year-old cathedral, their shells causing damage which took twenty years to repair.

Now the wrecked streets have been rebuilt, the bombed-out areas transformed into beautiful parks, children's playgrounds and blocks of new apartment houses with swimming pools, modern laundries, gymnasiums, lecture halls, libraries and nurseries. Oh, yes, I mustn't forget to mention that those *"verfluchte Sozies"* are running Vienna again. The city is rapidly becoming again one of Europe's musical, cultural and scientific centers, attracting growing numbers of tourists from all over the world.

Years of violent internal strife, disillusionment with Greater Germany, humiliation, defeat and ten years of occupation by the victorious Allies were the prerequisites for this new orientation. Crowned by the good fortune of a peace treaty Vienna, after forty years of confusion and lack of direction, is coming into its own. Its language and culture are becoming integrated with those of the minority leftovers of the old Empire, creating a new Vienna with its own unique characteristics.

The language is German—but is it? The Viennese carefully emphasize the differences and Germans have a hard time understanding it. The renowned Viennese kitchen marries the *Wiener Zuckerbäcker* with *Carlsbad Oblatten*, Hungarian sausage and goulash, Czech Knödeln, German frankfurters—to the tune of Viennese folk music mingling with the passionate strains of Hungarian gypsy violins. Efficient Czech tailors are next-door-neighbors to shops featuring the many regional costumes of the provinces. Everything from the former farflung Empire is represented and all of it spells the new Vienna.

How do we feel about it now? Our dear uncle is no longer there but some members of our families return for occasional visits. So shall we. We will enjoy the magnificent opera, which is better than ever, the folk music, the theatre, the organ concerts in the Stephanskirche, the charming dinners in the Kerzenstüberl, the museums, the walks in the beautiful parks, the Hauptallee, the Wienerwald. Yet we will never want to be anything but American tourists revisiting an old, charming and familiar city.

XXIV. TRAVEL WITH CHILDREN

We love to travel with our children. It wouldn't be half so nice without them. They seem to enjoy it too. Some years ago we sat with a group of friends in a cafe in Copenhagen. The discussion centered around the pros and cons of traveling with children. One parent remarked, "I can hardly wait until they're old enough to travel on their own."

Lorraine and Barbara exchanged glances. Later that night there was a knock at our door. There were the girls, in their robes, looking very serious. "Tell me," said the little one, obviously worried, "we would like to know, when we are old enough to travel on our own, couldn't we still go with you? . . . You're such good company."

Well, as you see, we still do. And when we won't anymore, it always will be a pleasure to remember the fun we had together. They are interested, helpful, sometimes—as all children—unbearable, most of the time truly good company.

Lorraine, our youngest, was barely eight years old when we took her on our first big trip. She was small for her age with tiny, slender hands which liked to be cuddled. Her inimitable sense of humor and her forthrightness were often a great help in awkward situations.

Many years ago, on a visit to Venice, we stayed in one of those fancy new hotels catering to Americans. Meals were included in the very high prices. The food was bad and the service poor, but with our European upbringing since we were paying for our meals, we felt we just had to eat there. One does not waste food! We felt cheated, angry and depressed.

The only redeeming feature was the amusing view from our windows. Looking out over the main entrance, we could see the many gondolas discharging streams of American tourists. (Suckers!) It was fun to watch how awkwardly the stiffly-

74

corseted women—loaded down with enormous handbags, cameras and whatnot—managed to get out of the swaying, wobbly gondolas. I'm sure we were not alone in wondering, waiting, rather maliciously hoping... When...? Which one ...? But as it happened, it was only in Norway that I helped fish a middle-aged schoolteacher out of the cold water.

After a second meal in our hotel, the children declared firmly that they would not set foot in that dining room again. Neither explanations nor threats had any effect. Marianne and I continued to eat in the dining room alone, wishing we had as much guts as the kids. Filled with mounting anger toward the hotel, the travel agent and even the pigeons in the Piazza San Marco we were about ready to explode when Lorraine spoke up: "Is this any way to treat a child? I'm hungry and I didn't come to Venice to eat roast beef; I want spaghetti."

How she determined that the awful meat served us was roast beef I don't know, but her words worked magic. Throwing economy to the winds, we never ate in the hotel again and from then on, we managed to have a delightful time in Venice.

XXV. REUNION BEHIND THE IRON CURTAIN

It was in 1958, two years after the Hungarian uprising against its Communist regime that I had visited Budapest for the first time since leaving Europe in 1935. My oldest sister was still living there. Remember her? She was the one who frightened the German officers when they came to call on her more than fifty years before.

I wanted very much to see her but we had no visa and I wasn't sure it was advisable for us to go. The American Consulate in Vienna didn't see any reason why we shouldn't and referred us to the official Hungarian travel agency. Within a few days, we received a visa for a weekend visit which included travel by bus, hotel and meals.

Early that Saturday morning we took our places in a comfortable bus filled mainly with Hungarians from far and wide returning to visit relatives. Others, like the French family sitting next to us, were tourists eager to take a peek behind the Iron Curtain.

It was with some trepidation that we approached the Hungarian border, about an hour's drive away. The Austrian guards passed us through quickly and a short distance further on, we were on Hungarian soil. The electric gates were closed and soldiers with tommyguns surrounded our bus. All luggage had to be taken off the bus and all the passengers lined up in a special room for passport and luggage inspection. It wasn't too different from going through customs in the States except for the soldiers with their guns and a world of difference in the atmosphere.

The officials were correct, unsmiling and quite efficient. I watched through a window as two guards went carefully through the pockets and lining of the coat I had left hanging in the bus. When luggage and passengers were finally resettled, an officer entered with our passports and slowly, with a look of disapproval and mistrust, handed each one back to its owner. It was obvious that he understood German; nevertheless he addressed us in Hungarian, knowing that many of the people didn't understand a word. Echoes of the officers of the old Empire—only the whip across the face was missing!

Finally, we were on our way again. The ravages of the war were visible everywhere but nowhere to the same extent as in Budapest, where we arrived some three hours later. There wasn't an undamaged building to be seen. Block after block of apartment houses, as well as many famous landmarks, had been completely wiped out by months of siege, air raids, and heavy artillery barrages across the Danube between the Germans and the Russians. Added to this was the new damage inflicted during the 1956 uprising on whatever buildings had been repaired or rebuilt after the war.

My brother-in-law, then in his seventies, had come to meet us at the hotel. My sister was waiting for us at home, he said. We exchanged embraces for the first time since 1935, and for the first time they were introduced to my wife and children. My sister had been a vivacious, creative human being—an excellent speaker, a gifted writer and educator. Now, big and extremely fat, with painfully swollen feet, she remained seated at the window of the room in which she had been locked up with eighteen others during the Nazi days, awaiting deportation. She told me she had not been outside her apartment in two years.

The table was set for lunch, with all the delicacies she knew I had loved as a youngster . . . goose livers, smoked goose, the famous Hungarian salami, cold cherry soup—enough to feed two dozen people. She was the respected matriarch of the neighborhood and her friends had collected all the delicacies they could find, legally or illegally, in our honor. Happy, tear-stained, she pointed to the table and said: "I told you when you called from Vienna not to bring anything. *The only need we have is food* and, as you see, we have everything." My brother-in-law, noticing my glance around the room, said: "Oh, my books? I gave them all away. We really don't need them."

With a sudden, involuntary motion, I reached into my pocket and offered him my fountain pen. He thanked me but said, "I really don't need it. I have one, found it on the street," pointing to a broken plastic pencil. (He was wearing a suit I had sent him shortly after the war.)

We listened to their flat, unconvincing descriptions of all the "wonderful changes, the new life, the bright future." Of course they would never leave, they said. This was their country, their city, where they had spent the better part of their lives, working and teaching. The longer we listened, the more it depressed us and the more clearly I could see again the words another sister had written after the war: "I envy those who have been murdered; they don't have to live with what we have seen."

Friends and neighbors dropped in during the afternoon, bringing gifts—a little vase, a figurine—sharing their few remaining treasures from a better past. We toured the city in buses and streetcars and went for long walks on the Margareten Insel. My sister never joined us, just stood at the window, watching. There were thousands of people in the coffee houses, filling all the chairs in the parks, overflowing the churches as they attended Sunday Mass. They all looked well fed, but shabby. I tried to talk to some of them but they would not respond—to a stranger with well-dressed children . . .

Sunday night we exchanged our last goodbyes. My sister

died a few months later—the first natural death in the family in 29 years!

We joined a silent group in our bus, driving through the dark night. "Shall we talk?" asked the young Frenchman. There was no answer. It was not until the last Hungarian gate closed behind us that we all suddenly felt free to converse. It was terrifying to realize that until then we had been afraid to say anything, afraid even of each other. I asked my children a few days later, when we were back in Vienna, what had been their impression of our Budapest visit. "We never saw anybody smile," they said.

Well, you will be interested to know, that today we returned from another weekend in Budapest, the first since 1958. We went to see my youngest sister who had moved there from Rumania several years before.

Crossing the Hungarian border has changed considerably. Now there is friendliness, laughter, practically no customs inspection. You don't have to talk to the guards or get out of the bus if you don't want to. Yet one thing has not changed— the physical evidence of the Iron Curtain.

After the last guard left our bus, the electrically-operated gate opened to let us through. As far as the eye can see there are tall, barbed-wire fences guarded by towers bristling with machine guns and automatic rifles. Between each fence is a "no-man's land"—about a hundred feet in width, cleared of all trees and brush, the soil so freshly plowed that even a rabbit's footsteps show. The fact that this fertile Hungarian soil, which has been producing food and maintaining life for hundreds of years, is being used to set murderous traps is a nightmare even more depressing than the tommyguns and barbed wire.

An attractive young woman speaking several languages joined us at the border. She was to be our "guide" until the bus crossed the border again on the way back. She was an attorney trying to make some extra money. She had visited some of the other Iron Curtain countries but had never been outside them, not even to nearby Vienna. "We don't trust each other, you see," she explained.

"We don't trust each other!" This is the tragic reality which divides nations and millions of people all over the world; which encourages the ever-accelerating production of unimaginably destructive weapons; which renders life itself on our planet so dangerously precarious.

Every few thousand feet for miles and miles there are soldiers walking in pairs on the highway or lying among the bushes, guns pointed toward the road or toward where, across the Danube just a mile or two away, lies Czechoslovakia, another border of mistrust . . .

My sister had been only 15 years old when I had last seen her 35 years ago. It was heartwarming to be with her again and to greet my two nephews—one a surgeon, the other an engineer (aged six and two when I had last seen them). Their late teens were spent in concentration camps in Germany and as mine workers in Poland. In the chaos of the last months of the war, they had escaped from a labor camp and, speaking fluent French, had been adopted by some French prisoners working nearby. Freed by the advancing Allied armies, they had been spared the last-minute-frenzy of extermination.

My nephew the surgeon reminded me that several years earlier he had had an irresistable desire to talk to me. A telephone call from Eastern Europe to the U.S.A.! It had taken him three months to get a permit and almost three months' salary to pay for the call. He had waited at the phone for hours. Finally, the call came through. His wife and child sat motionless beside him, holding their breaths. At last he heard my voice, thousands of miles and years away. Choking with emotion, hardly able to speak, what do you suppose he said? "What time is it now in Los Angeles?" And believe it or not, I answered in kind.

All too soon it was time again to make our farewells. And at the border we said goodbye to our attractive guide. We felt sad to leave her there, having to walk five miles back to the nearest town. The border guards had bicycles; she did not.

In a few days we shall leave for Israel to visit another one of my sisters who survived Hitler. Another difficult reunion after so many many years of separation!

Israel

XXVI. WHAT IF THE ARABS...

We left Vienna for Israel about a week ago on an El-Al Airlines plane. More than half the passengers were immigrants from Eastern Europe, boarding a plane for the first time. Some were enthusiastic young people but more were old men and women, whose hardships of life were engraved in the deep wrinkles of their suntanned faces and in the rough, hard skin of their hands. They had been decimated and uprooted many times and now they were here, looking forward with anxious expectations to their future in the Biblical Land.

My family and I were eagerly anticipating our stop in Istanbul, a city which held for me all the fantasies created by the books I had read as a youngster about the fabulous mysteries of the Orient, its treasures and its harems, to which Hungarian maidens had been abducted during the 150 years of Turkish occupation. Of course they were always rescued by a hero with whom a young boy could identify with great pleasure.

How disappointing it was to land some hours later at an airport far outside the city with not a minaret in sight, nor even a single Turk sporting a fez. Our flight was behind schedule; we weren't even allowed to leave the plane. Sitting at the window, I watched the few passengers who were boarding, among them one who could be a Turk! He wore a little straw hat and looked small carrying a large shopping net overflowing with packages. Well, Istanbul was not a total loss after all.

He sat down next to Barbara and began a lively conversation in English, French and German. It didn't take long to discover that he was not a Turk but a Hungarian, born near my birthplace, and that his name was also Friedman. Curiously enough, there were half a dozen other Friedmans on the plane, none of

80

The Grossglockner, highest mountain in Austria

Above the glacier of the Grossglockner

Benedictine Monk and the Grossglockner

Hallstatt, Austria

The house Böck, our hotel in Hallstatt

Marianne in Hallstatt

Near Hallstatt

Hiking near Kitzbühel, Austria

Near Kitzbühel

On the high summer meadow

Sonje Fjord in Norway

Fisherman's lookout in Norway

Summer in Norway

The flower market in Bergen

Jeremiah by Max Band

them related to me. We arrived in Israel late at night. Our Mr. Friedman from Istanbul waited until he was sure we were taken care of, then gave me his card and asked that we call him when we got to Jerusalem.

My sister and brother-in-law were waiting for us. After a three-hour drive in an ancient taxi big enough to hold eight people, we arrived at their home in this small town near Haifa. It was pitch dark, very hot and humid. Undoubtedly, August is always hot in Israel but we had to come in August during a heat wave!

My sister has a charming little house with a large garden full of fruit trees and flowers. It has a living room, a sleeping porch, kitchen and an unfinished bathroom. Quite an achievement this house for an old couple who came here 15 years ago after receiving a last beating "for deserting their European homeland!"

They had started life in this land in a hut on a hillside, with a stone for a hammer, their only property the clothing on their backs and photographs tracing our family back for generations. How she did it I don't know, but my sister had hung on to them somehow—in jails, in hiding, in flights across pathless mountains and during her long, hopeless search for her little girl, her only child, killed by the Nazis.

Those first months must have been terribly difficult. It took quite some time before help from me was able to reach them. Meanwhile, my sister was busily growing vegetables, raising chickens and milking the goat which shared their hut. My brother-in-law, 60 years old at the time, his leg crippled by experimental surgery performed on him in a concentration camp, did road work, breaking stones and mixing cement.

You should see the letters she sent us during those months, scribbled in pencil on scraps of paper. Not a word about their hardships but glowing with enthusiasm for their new country, the beauty of its landscapes, the miracles transforming it, their joyous hopes and plans. Above everything else, she wrote something I shall never forget, something that should be engraved on the minds and hearts of all the anxious, terrified millions of human beings in our troubled world:

81

"For months after we arrived," she wrote, "I was haunted by a feeling I could not identify. I fell asleep with it after the day's hard work and woke with it each morning to the first rays of the rising sun. It was a good feeling but so new to me that only gradually I came to recognize it for what it was. You see, for the first time in my life I was living without fear."

At this point, I must tell you that I had set out on this first journey to Israel with some apprehension and a gnawing feeling of resentment. The resentment I am sure stemmed from my lifelong opposition to supernationalism—the breeding ground of so much bigotry, hate and violence throughout history, as I knew only too well from my own life experience. And yet, why was this feeling so strong in relation to Israel when I am convinced that without this intense nationalism Israel would never have come into existence and could not possibly survive today.

My reactions became clearer to me one day during a visit to the Friedmans in their lovely home in Jerusalem. My hosts were about my age, born near the city of my birth. They had come to what was then Palestine in their early teens. One of their sons was present with his wife and child, all born in this country—and with a friend, a young man in his twenties, a refugee from the 1956 Hungarian uprising. We were deeply engaged in a discussion about the status, security and future of Israel. In the course of it, the young man asked: "What will happen to us if all the Arab countries, with their growing military power, attack us again?" Impatiently our host replied: "After living in Israel for five years how can you even ask such a question? How can you possibly be afraid?"

Suddenly I was not in Jerusalem but back in my home-town half a century earlier. It was snowing and freezing cold. Fur cap pulled deep down over my head, flaps covering my ears, my hand tucked into my father's fur glove, we were on our way to a meeting. I knew most of the men and the few other boys who were there. The room was noisy with conversation. The center of attention was a group of young men in their teens who were planning to emigrate to Palestine. The older men clustered around them, encouraging and blessing them, praising their mission to restore the greatness of ancient Judea, to return the Promised Land to "God's Chosen People."

And then it happened. My father rose. He dropped his contribution toward the journey as had all the others into a metal container. He expressed his agreement with the necessity of establishing a Jewish state and his respect for those who supported this goal on religious grounds. However, he felt they ought to discuss some of the realistic difficulties involved. "What if those powerful Arab nations..." He was never allowed to finish his question. Decades later, a young man in Jerusalem did that. My father was denounced as a godless unbeliever who dared to question the will of the Almighty and the rights of the children of Israel.... With a few well-chosen Biblical quotations of the Learned, and with some not-so-Biblical but highly descriptive and powerful expressions of others hurled at us, we were out in the deep snow again, far away from the phantasy of the warm Land of Plenty.

I could never decide which of my feelings was the more powerful—my pride in my father for speaking or my anger at him for the humiliating scene that followed. Obviously my father was in the wrong. Without the fanatical faith of those early pioneers there would be no state of Israel today.

XXVII. NAZARETH

The last few days have been so hot that we questioned whether we should hide from the burning sun and stay at home or go sightseeing and try to forget about it. Either way, there was no escaping it. It was as hot in the shade as in the sun, walking or standing still, and it didn't cool off at night. Nevertheless, we hired a large, rickety taxi and set out.

Our native-born driver understood and spoke English quite well except when he preferred not to. The first day he drove us north. After a short stop in Nazareth, he proceeded across an endless stretch of deserted-looking wasteland baking in the sun. It was no longer a miracle to me that the Jews, fleeing from Egypt, baked their unleavened bread on their backs. The miracle was that it did not burn to a crisp.

We passed a couple of broken-down abandoned taxis and

noticed with discomfort that they didn't look much worse than ours. I thought about the friends back in the States who had advised us not to order a car ahead of time. "If you want one, you can probably get it at Haifa," they said. If I tell you that the brand new, air-conditioned cars that passed us occasionally are available if ordered in advance, that they don't cost as much as I paid for our rickety hearse, you will understand why my thoughts about our advisers are not fit for international correspondence.

No amount of protest from my sister could stop the driver from going where he wanted to go. He not only forgot English, but also his native Hebrew. He landed us in Tiberias, way below sea level and unbearably hot, deposited us on one of the public beaches and suggested we spend the day there. Then he made off toward a group of enthusiastic friends and disappeared among the hundreds of swimmers. The temperature continued to rise steadily. Finally, after hours of argument, disgruntled because we had spoiled his day, he consented to drive us home. For the next two days, we decided to do our sightseeing at night, and on the third day, with the early sunrise we were on our way to Jerusalem.

But let me tell you first about Nazareth. It is very much as I imagined it must have been 2,000 years ago, especially once you get to the narrow streets of steps, with donkeys the only transportation. From a distance, you see an ancient market with its pottery-makers, blacksmiths and all the other craftsmen of a bygone era. It is only when you get into the middle of the market that you notice the plastic toys and dishes, the piles of empty cans and other such signs of our modern civilization. The Arabs look timeless sitting on their little donkeys, except that now they wear blue jeans and, occasionally tennis shoes.

There was one impression which was more powerful than any other. It was vague then but it is becoming clearer every day. Israel is the first country I have ever been in where the present, the Bible, history, fact and fantasy not only live side by side but are so fused that it is almost impossible to separate them. Both the Jewish and the Christian guides who show you

84

the Biblical sites talk of them as present-day realities, inter-mingling historical facts, religious beliefs and miracles without so much as a change of voice.

The longer I am here the more I am impressed by the contradictions which exist alongside each other without apparent conflict—as they do in the Unconscious of the individual or as reality, fantasy and dreams are interwoven without sharp delineation in children and old people.

XXVIII. THE CAVES OF ELIJAH

One of the memorable experiences to date was our visit to the Caves of the Prophet Elijah, the night before we left for Jerusalem. It was almost dark when our driver called for us. We drove first to Haifa, a teeming and steaming port city where, as in so much of Israel, the ancient and the modern blend imper-ceptibly into each other. We ascended to the very top of Mount Carmel, the beautiful residential district perched high above the city and the harbor. The view is spectacular—the sparkling lights of the city and the shoreline, the illuminated ships on the horizon merging with the myriad stars in the dark Mediter-ranean sky.

On our way down we called on a distant relative who had become an influential man in Haifa. Now a head taller than I, I had seen him last about 40 years before when, as a youngster, he was leaving for Palestine with his brother. He and his family live in a modern apartment on one of the steep streets on Mount Carmel. The traffic is extremely heavy, as it is in all the large cities of Israel and the noise is disturbing enough to interfere with conversation. The old residents are pleased by Haifa's rapid growth in recent years but there is also nos-talgia for the quiet and privacy of earlier times and a pride in the ancient historical background of the city. As our hostess expressed it, almost screaming to be heard over the noise of shifting gears, "We like Haifa because it is so old and quiet. Tel-Aviv is so new and noisy that we just couldn't live there."

Late that night we walked up the steep approach to the Caves of Elijah in the midst of a beautiful, well-kept park.

Upon entering them, history is turned back by milleniums. As in a fictional time-machine, you are carried back to pre-Christian times.

Cave after cave is filled with moaning, praying, sleeping people. Hundreds of candles glow all about you. Since ancient times the Caves have been credited with miraculous powers by Jews as well as Christians and Moslems. From near and far they come, sometimes walking for weeks, even months, bringing their sick, their incurables, their elders, their children. Entire families move into an available cave, eat, live and sleep there until a miracle works or . . . they must carry away their dead to make room for others.

The atmosphere is one of deep, unquestioning faith. Even the paid professionals who sell candles, serve as guides, offer prayers for the sick and dying are unobtrusive and sincere. It is possible that the lateness of the hour at which we visited the Caves contributed to the impressiveness of the scene, but a feeling of awe and mystery was inescapable. After all, no matter how old and mature we may have become, we were all children once and we all have an Unconscious—depository of the irrational, the magical, the belief in omnipotence and miracles which constantly affect our conscious life and thought.

As we left the Caves, my sister broke a small twig from a bush near the entrance and solemnly, with some instructions I did not hear, gave it to Marianne to protect us against illness, accident and bad fortune!

XXIX. DRIVING TO JERUSALEM

It was five o'clock in the morning and the sun was just rising when we said goodbye to my sister and brother-in-law before leaving for Tel-Aviv and Jerusalem. This was the most painful of the many farewells we had lived through on our journey. During the days we had spent with my sister, she had become increasingly depressed because the 35 years of separation, so crowded with world-shaking events and tragic personal experiences, could not be erased; that we could not return to our adolescence and be together to start life over again. Besides, she had fallen in love with Marianne and our daughters, whom she had never met before, and to part from them after so many partings was unbearable to her.

The air was almost cool for once and the road to Tel-Aviv beautiful—flanked by miles and miles of orchards, banana fields, historic landmarks and ruins of the old Roman Empire.

Our driver announced cheerfully, when we reached Tel-Aviv, that he was sure we would not mind if someone else drove us to Jerusalem because something was wrong with his car. He was a gonef (a cheat), charming and attractive to be sure, but still a gonef, who obviously had other plans for himself. He drove us around and pointed out the important landmarks. Tel-Aviv is a new city, in a big hurry to grow up, and it is not very attractive. Our contract with the rental company called for our spending most of the day in Tel-Aviv but we were glad when, after a short tour, he continued on through the narrow old streets of Jaffa to the company garage, eager to say good-bye to us and be off about his private pursuits.

I did not understand his heated discussions in Hebrew with the mechanics, but after a few trips around the block, frankly disappointed, he told us that they couldn't find anything wrong with the car. Nevertheless he predicted hopefully that his car would never make the steep road to Jerusalem. As a matter of fact, I still can't understand how the car ever carried us even one block and we would have been delighted to change, but apparently no other car or driver was available.

Off we went. Once fate decided against his plans, he was his old cheerful self again and seemed to enjoy the trip. We did too. It is a magnificent ride—first a wide freeway becoming as it nears Jerusalem an increasingly steep, winding mountain road. It goes through a narrow corridor (the only connecting link to Jerusalem) surrounded on all sides by Jordan. It leads through deep forests planted in the last 15 years, which have changed the landscape and the climate itself of Israel, producing wood for the future, top-soil, moisture to raise fruit and vegetables undreamed of on the barren hillsides before. It winds through young orchards and old olive groves—trees with giant trunks said to be more than a thousand years old.

Stone terraces built by the Romans are newly repaired and

functioning—holding the top-soil for trees and vines heavy with fruit. The Promised Land is a Land of Plenty wherever you look—but in the roadside ditches between the new trees of the forests, are the rusting, decaying torsos of armored cars and tanks—monuments of the War of Independence. Thousands of years of history within a few miles!

We reached Jerusalem in mid-morning. The first impression is overwhelming. We drove through broad avenues offering all the transportation facilities available in any big city today and lined with modern buildings, offices and department stores. But look down any of the narrow side streets and you are in the deepest Orient, with open-air markets stretching as far as the eye can see, a jumble of fruits, vegetables, meats, cooked foods, pottery, leather goods and jewelry fashioned by the famous Yemenite craftsmen.

You know by now that much as I love just to look at a foreign city, enjoy a work of art, the quiet solemnity of a beautiful church, the narrow trail through a silent dark forest, there is nothing that attracts me so much as people. People new to me and in their natural environment! And what better place than a market to observe the infinite variety of human nature?

Even in our modern cities markets are fascinating. Just spend a little time watching the shoppers in a self-service super-market and you will learn more about human beings than all the experimental laboratories can teach you. If you find your-self in a foreign land and want to know what its people are all about, if you really want to *be* with them, go to an open-air market. You don't have to understand one word of the lan-guage yet you will gain much insight into the life of Everyman.

Here you will find the merchant and the buyer: the aggres-sive persuaders shrewdly exploiting vanity; the bargain hunters; those who cannot deny themselves anything and those who never open their purses more than a crack. Here too are the cheats, the liars and the thieves, to say nothing of the beggars and those who respond to them out of generosity or guilt—or who wave them off with irritation or indifference. You see the well-to-do buying the best of everything and the poor haggling over the spoiling fruit and the string beans which bend but do not break.

Every walk of life, every character you have ever met or imagined, every feeling you like or dislike in yourself parades before you in seething action. Where better to see men, women and children dealing with such basic needs as food; to observe how well or badly they function within the framework of their society; to recognize man's need to communicate and to depend on his fellow man!

Well, as you see, I love markets—the more primitive, the more they delight and fascinate me, the more they make me feel at home, at one with the human race. Every simple stall manned by an entire family of Arabs or Oriental Jews frames a comedy or tragedy of such depth, such beauty or ugliness as has seldom been captured in books or on the stage.

However, if life in the raw repels you, don't go to a market, especially to an Oriental market. You will see only the filth, smell the stench, recoil from the sores of the sick. Your air-conditioned hotel is more refined, your room spotlessly clean and you can always lock the door against the world outside. If you are afraid of people as they are, afraid to see yourself as you really are rather than as you think you are or ought to be— if you prefer to see in life only the good and the beautiful, or if life represents to you only evil and ugliness—in other words, if you are afraid of the whole turbulent range of human experience, then don't ever go to see a great play either, or ever read a great book. They will disturb you just as profoundly as a visit to an Oriental market.

XXX. THE LIGHTS OF MOUNT SCOPUS

It was the height of luxury to walk into the spacious lobby of the Hotel King David. It was still hot, but the dry heat of high desert with a hint of cool breeze, becoming stronger at the end of the day. At night one must wear a jacket or sweater, and a blanket is a necessity. It took about two hours before our rooms were ready. Meanwhile, we made reservations for sight-seeing trips for the next three days and, as soon as we had cleaned up, we were out on the street.

89

We had walked only a couple of blocks when we were greeted with delight by none other than our Mr. Friedman from Istanbul. "I just came down to buy a book," he said, "but the store is closed. I have nothing to do and would be delighted to show you around." We accepted gladly. He led us to his new, air-conditioned car and, at my request, we were on our way to the most religious, Chassidic quarters of the city. Before we got there, our friend stopped at a store selling religious articles to buy me a skullcap. One is not allowed to walk in that quarter without a head-covering. At his call, a middle-aged man with a long beard and a cheerful face, looking like a Santa Claus, came out of the store with a silver-embroidered, black silk skullcap for me. You won't believe it but he also spoke Hungarian, was from near my birthplace and his name was Friedman!

We spent half the afternoon walking the streets, visiting places of worship and study, looking at the rows of apartments with cave-like entrances. We saw very few women—they withdraw at the sight of strangers. Men and boys all had long side-curls and wore skullcaps of infinite variety—small knitted ones on the youngsters, held in place with large bobby pins, while the old men wore black silk ones covered by hats as black as their long *caftans*. Young and old alike covered their eyes at the sight of strange women, and men as well as women hid their faces or turned away whenever I tried to take a picture.

In my childhood there was a large congregation of Chassidim in our city. How fascinated I was by their long silk gowns, round hats banded in fur, black mocassins and white socks! Occasionally, on holy days, my father took me to their synagogues to listen to their joyous singing, watch their religious dancing. Now, as we peered into synagogue windows, I wondered how many of these old men seated on benches around wooden tables, studying the Talmud or murmuring their prayers, might be those I had seen when they were children or young men going to their daily ritual baths or dressed elegantly in their silks on High Holy Days. Yes, how many?

The city of my birth was also a large Catholic center, the

90

site of a bishopric with a magnificent palace and garden. Catholic priests and nuns were as much a part of the street scene as the Chassidim. I was as familiar with the interiors of the Catholic churches as with the synagogues, or the services in a certain Protestant church where one of my most gifted friends, at the age of 12, played the organ. He became a brilliant musician with a great future as a composer until he was incinerated in a German concentration camp. My strong interest in the arts and the theatre also dates back to those early years of my life I spent in the nursery school of a Catholic convent.

Now, for the first time since those long-gone days, I was seeing Chassidic Jews and Catholic priests existing peaceably side by side and sharing the daily life of a city without visible conflict.

Later on, Mr. Friedman drove us to the Hebrew University. It is a beautifully-planned modern campus already finding it difficult to accommodate the thousands of students from all parts of the world. Hard to believe it is only about a decade old, having been constructed after the War of Independence. The old university on Mount Scopus was not only largely destroyed by shells but was completely lost to education since it was situated in the center of the Old City and until June of 1967 was in the hands of the Arabs.

Even though it was in Jordanian territory and unusable, it belonged to Israel according to the truce provisions. It was guarded by a small garrison of Israeli soldiers, changed every few weeks under the protection of the United Nations truce team. Two strong lights, burning all night at the old university, sent the message from Mount Scopus that all was well. Everybody in Jerusalem knew that if those lights ever went out, there was danger, serious danger not only for the small garrison but for all Jerusalem, all Israel.

All this changed, of course, after the summer of 1967.

XXXI. "ALLE MENSCHEN WERDEN BRÜDER"

We have seen a lot in the last few days. I have mentioned several times how ancient and modern, historical and Biblical blend into each other in Israel. Nowhere is this more apparent than in Jerusalem. All in all, I have seen many cities in many lands, have strong affection for them, but the impact of Jerusalem is unique.

Our hotel is elegant and spacious, full of tourists of all faiths from all parts of the world. It is a pity that most people who come to Israel, especially from the United States, are advised by many tourist agencies to stay in Tel-Aviv. Jerusalem is far superior in every respect. Its climate is much more agreeable and it offers excellent accommodations, breathtaking views, indescribably lovely colors.

Our balcony overlooks the old walled city across the no-man's land just a few hundred yards away. It is one of those sights no one who has ever seen it can forget. The first building to the right is the Tomb of King David, said to be about 3,000 years old. Next to it is the Sanhedrin, the more than 2,000-year-old High Court. King David's Tomb is accessible from Israel and attracts innumerable tourists. Then come buildings of every shape, on all levels, built of the same solid stone as the high walls, which look like natural outgrowths of the massive rocks of the hills of Jerusalem. They remind one of groups of crystals differentiated out of rocks, or of sculpture growing out of an unhewn base. One could sit here for hours, watching the ever-changing lights, shadows and colors.

It is still dark when I wake up in the morning, and am drawn to the balcony. The city is dark, a giant, solid rock. Gradually, vague outlines of buildings take shape against the sky. The lights from Mount Scopus, from the high towers manned by Arab guards look like big bright stars among the other stars. They fade out together as the rays of the rising sun color the sky. Building after building slowly becomes distinct, light and shade playing over the yellow-white stone, like the flickering flames of ancient oil lamps.

Like a ballet on a dark stage. The dancers rise, turning slowly one by one to single notes, at the command of a magical baton. As the stage slowly lights up, more dancers appear, accompanied by chords of increasing crescendo. They merge into a large group, twirling to the rhythm of muted woodwinds and

92

massed strings. Then, as the sun bursts through with blinding intensity, the scene grows to a magnificent frenzy, to the sound of trumpets ... the trombones in Aida ... the *"Alle Menschen Werden Brüder ..."* of Beethoven's Ninth Symphony.

XXXII. SIX MILLION MURDERED

For the past two days we have been touring in and around Jerusalem in sightseeing buses, sometimes with dozens of other people, occasionally with just our guides, who are old friends by now. Just a few miles in any direction and there is the Jordanian border with its barbed wire, machine-gun nests and hidden guards. You don't actually see them but a few steps in the wrong direction into no-man's land and .... Once again two worlds are separated from each other by hate and violence. How tragic when their joint effort could so easily change the face of a continent, feed all the hungry, shelter the homeless, cure the sick!

I have never seen a border like this one; it circles the entire territory belonging to Israel. You do not need barbed wire or special markings to recognize the borders; the lines are sharply drawn by Israel's dedication to using human energy productively. Hillsides and valleys are planted with trees; luscious orchards fill the stone terraces; men and women with tractors are at work in the fields; sprinklers continually irrigate valleys where armies fought for thousands of years for possession of a water-well. Abruptly, trees, orchards and green fields end at the Arab borders. Beyond ... no trucks, no tractors, no people at work ... just desolation. Here and there you see a cluster of stone dwellings difficult to differentiate from the barren, rocky hillsides—Biblical towns, sites of ancient and modern battles.

We visited Ein Karem, the birthplace of John the Baptist and drank the cool water from the deeply hidden wells. We admired the churches which had been built and rebuilt by Christian "believers" and by the Crusaders—and which had been plundered and destroyed over and over again by "unbelievers"—pagans, Moslems and the "believers" of other faiths. Differences in the size and color of the stones bear witness to the history of centuries. The larger and yellower they are, the older they are.

What passion, what energy it must have taken to build them; what fury and urge to destroy these solid stone buildings ... without so much as a stick of dynamite!

We have seen the Dead Sea Scrolls, visited the Church of the Visitation and many other Roman Catholic and Greek Orthodox churches, the Cathedral of Richard the Lion-Hearted and the temple in the Hadassah Hospital (where we watched a joyous young father receive his first-born under the Chagall windows); ancient excavations; modern villages of new immigrants; and the "round stones" mentioned in the Bible.

For a long, long time nobody knew what the Bible was referring to until one such stone was discovered in an excavation within walking distance of our hotel. They are like large millstones rolled and fitted into the entrances of caves where the dead were buried. The stones served a double purpose of preventing the dead from getting out and the living from getting in to rob the graves. They had many other ingenious devices for that purpose which could have been early models for the big, round steel doors of our bank vaults today. It seems we haven't come very far since those ancient times, either in the matter of modifying man's urge to steal or in devising means of protection against it.

One day our guides took us to the memorial for the six million Jews murdered by the Nazis. They left us at the entrance and waited for us at the far exit. You are alone—as one must be alone in this place. No one talks—the silence is deafening. They are all there, from every country, from every city, town or village you ever heard of. Photographs, posters, extermination orders, lamp shades made of human skin, soap made of human fat, vests made of the yellow parchment of Holy Scriptures, a bloody prayer shawl, and a bullet-riddled Torah—accusing witnesses to a brutality that staggers the imagination and deadens the heart.

And the photographs ... the thousands of photographs of the emaciated, the mutilated, the diseased, the dead! Suddenly you realize that you are not just looking, you are searching

94

with dread for those who were yours, terrified that you just might . . . just as you did in 1945 when our Army was sending back the first films from the concentration camps.

As we walked silently down the well-kept paths to rejoin our guides, we saw an old gardener carefully tending his flowers and a younger one standing in a ditch, his long beard covering his bare chest, perspiration pouring down his face, his bronzed, muscular arms swinging a heavy pickaxe into the solid rock of Jerusalem. His greeting of "Shalom" and his infectious smile recalled us to present reality.

Looking at him, thinking of the hundreds of thousands like him who are recreating Israel, you are swept by a feeling that those six million live again in the remnants who have come from the prisons, ghettos and persecutions of Europe and many other lands. They live again in the Oriental Jewish nomads who through centuries of oppression were a total loss to humanity and have now become farmers, independent artisans, craftsmen and scholars.

XXXIII. LAST DAY IN JERUSALEM AND THE "EXODUS" AT LYDDA

The night before we left Jerusalem we attended an informal song-and-dance evening at the Art Center near our hotel. We enjoyed the ancient ballads, their sadness vanquished by the fiery and funny songs of the new Israel, but nothing impressed us so much as the dancers—six young couples, as attractive and graceful as I have seen anywhere.

The crowd encircling the floor was large, leaving them little room. Their costumes were simple. There was no special lighting, no orchestra, just an accordion player. They performed ritual dances celebrating weddings and other festivities of bygone times. Everything they did was an expression of pure joy—joy of the spirit and joy of beautiful bodies in inspired motion.

Before the evening was over, the entire audience had joined them. Everybody, young and old, was dancing—elegant dresses from many lands mingling with the shorts and sports shirts of the Sabras and the native costumes of African students and diplomats. Jews and Christians, tourists from all parts of the world, joined hands ... *"Alle Menschen werden Brüder ... alle Menschen ... alle Menschen."*

It was midnight by the time we walked back to our hotel and our air-conditioned limousine would be waiting at sunrise to take us to the airport at Lydda, two hours away.

A last look from the balcony at the glowing Old City, motionless lips forming the often repeated words: "We'll be back" and we're on our way, down to steep winding road, through orchards and forests and ancient olive groves. Our driver, a middle-aged man, was full of information. A very early immigrant, he had been a policeman for many years under the British Mandate. He knew every hill, every path, practically every tree. He told us about the early struggles, the hardships, the bloody battles, the ambush killings which never stopped. He spoke with pride about the aspirations and achievements of his family and his nation.

Suddenly, Marianne pointed to a group of camels silhouetted against the horizon. There were about 20 of them, standing motionless—some in pairs, facing each other, heads high, cheeks almost touching; others in groups of three or four. Two Arab women dressed in black squatted motionless beside them. We paused for a long time, watching. It was a beautiful sight.

The discussion with our driver turned to Bersheba in the southern desert, another city where ancient and modern co-exist, where Arab and Jewish cultures live side by side without conflict. Bersheba, among other things, is famous for its camel market, but that's not all. It is also a marketplace for sheep, goats and wives, in that order—offered for exchange or sale—an ancient custom of the Atayeh, a Bedouin tribe, unchanged to this day.

With my family's interest in everything alive and our common fascination with markets, you can imagine that we had tried to arrange to visit Bersheba. Unfortunately, the camel-goat-wife market takes place only once a week, early on Thursday mornings, and we were unable to manage it unless we cancelled our trip to Rome. Bersheba will have to wait till we come again and, since its customs have persisted this long, it is

Venice at dusk

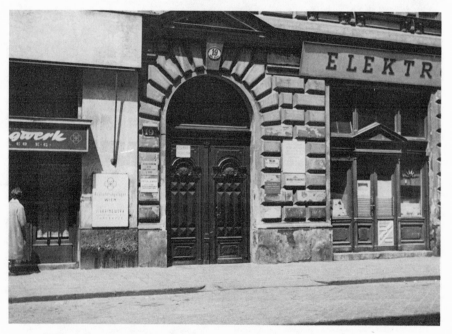

Wien, Berggasse 19, the home of Sigmund Freud until 1938

The statue of Freud in the Hall of Fame
of the University of Vienna

Ernest Jones unveiling the Centennial Plaque on Freud's
home in London, May 6, 1956

My sister's home in Israel

Street in the Chassidic section of Jerusalem
with the Chassidic University

The tomb of King David in Jerusalem

Ancient solid rock building
in Jerusalem

The Colosseum in Rome

Fi-Fi and her Mickey Mouse
with the chewed up nose

Walking through the ruins of ancient Rome

Fountain in front of St. Peters Cathedral, Rome

Pietà by Michelangelo

reasonable to expect that they won't change in my lifetime—although I have heard that the camels, at least, are being transported by trucks these days.

Finally we arrived at Lydda Airport. The noisiest Oriental market place could not compete with the babble of tongues, the confusion, the pushing and shoving which swallowed us up. Most people have some anxiety about flying, especially in foreign countries where they don't speak the language and are faced with unfamiliar customs. The experience at Lydda was fantastic, hilarious beyond description. I can't remember ever having seen so many people at any one airport ... all frantically rushing about in a mad scramble to locate their planes. There must have been 50 chartered planes scheduled to leave within minutes of each other. It looked like a general exodus; thousands of people grimly fighting for the last seats before it is too late, before everything is lost. Boarding that famous train in 1914, when thousands were actually left behind, did not compare with this; at least we all spoke the same language!

Our driver had talked one of the porters into taking our luggage. No small miracle! Who wants to handle the luggage for four people? The five of us, loaded to our necks, formed an irresistable wedge and, with our porter out front pushing, arguing, persuading, we finally reached a baggage counter. He piled up our suitcases among dozens of others, surrounded by trunks, sacks, baskets, shopping bags.

It had taken us about 15 minutes to negotiate 15 yards through angry men, hysterical mothers and crying children. I gave the porter a lavish tip for his heroic efforts, only to be told by stern officials, the moment he had disappeared into the crowd, that putting *any* luggage where ours was piled up was prohibited. Furthermore, this was the wrong counter—we must remove it without delay.

I'll never know how but we finally persuaded another porter to help us. By this time we were sure we would never see half our luggage again and that we would never make the plane. Somehow, though, we managed to get through customs, passport and currency control, checked in our luggage and, after

97

being propelled through several gates by the onrushing, yelling crowd, found ourselves being pushed up some steps and stuffed into the rear door of a plane. We could only hope it would turn out to be the one bound for Rome but we had no further choice in the matter and were so prostrated that none of us really cared. Two hours had gone by since we had left our air-conditioned limousine. It was now mid-morning and the heat wave had not subsided.

Miraculously we were on the right plane, but this was not the end of the fun. Neither the signs in three languages, nor the pleading of our stewardesses to "fasten your seat belts" discouraged the passengers from walking around, looking for friends and family, congratulating one another for having made it, putting up and pulling down hand luggage—often too heavy to lift.

The roar of the jet engines finally accomplished what no pleading had succeeded in doing. The natural anxiety of the take-off eventually glued people to their seats and we were off. We were then served an excellent lunch and at last there was peace and quiet. The air was so clear that we could see Cyprus, the Greek Islands, the Italian countryside, Naples, finally, the landmarks of Rome—as clearly as if we had a relief map at our fingertips.

Rome

XXXIV. ROME AND JERUSALEM

The Eternal City affords an interesting contrast to Jerusalem, the Holy City. Both were centers of culture long before the advent of Christianity—but such different cultures! Rome was the center of military power, dedicated to the pursuit of conquest, war, subjugation, slavery. Rome glorified violence in war and violence purely for pleasure at home. The magnificent Colosseum was sometimes used for chariot races and other competitive sports, but most of the time simply and exclusively to provide the Roman citizens of all classes with their pleasure in violence, in killing, with the enjoyment in watching the pain, the terror, the agony of dying.

The Colosseum is in ruins, a relic of ancient history, but the bullfight arenas are not; neither is the commercial exploitation of brutality for entertainment.

It is impossible not to draw the parallel. The idea of entertainment is emphasized by all; there was insistence on skill and courage in the fights of the gladiators and certainly an important requirement for a toreador, even if the moment of truth is the killing.

What about the killers in our present day entertainment? A gladiator with such lack of skill, lack of imagination and cowardice would have been sold as a beast of burden; a toreador laughed out of the arena, sent back to cleaning the stables. More is expected even of the bull that wants to be killed with honor, than of the mugs, the jailbirds, the sex-killers, the mobsters, the morons, the cowards in the dark and all the other artistic creations crowding our commercial entertainment media.

The Romans were at least honest; they loved, glorified war, killing, without any pretense of art or culture. They didn't

99

even try to sell deodorants or certain brand of togas. They did wear tunics, but no three-way stretch toga foundations.

"This is what people want," the writers, the producers say. "You are the one," they tell me, "who says that violence is in the nature of man." Yes, it is. But the function of education, of civilization, of culture is to modify it, neutralize it, use its energy for productive purposes, not cultivate brutality, reinforce it, exploit it. To call sheer brutality art because it shows human nature at its worst, entertainment because people watch it, is utter nonsense. After this excursion in our present civilization, let us go back to Rome.

Across the street from the Colosseum—if you can make it through the racing Fiats and motor scooters—is the Forum, where one can walk for hours among the ruins of ancient Rome. The temples, statues, public buildings, the magnificent arches erected to the glory of returning heroes who had destroyed ancient cities and cultures, burned irreplaceable libraries and works of art, looted treasure, killed enemy soldiers and civilians, dragging the enslaved survivors back to Rome in chains, to be exposed to the ridicule and violence of the jubilating crowds.

How splendid the celebrated hero, erect in his golden chariot, head crowned with laurel, victorious steel sparkling in the sun! Here are the ruined temples where they offered sacrifices to the gods for victory. There is the Senate where the august senators proclaimed the hero a Caesar, a God, an Emperor, and where the same august senators, on one Ides of March, thrust their steel into the anointed body of their greatest Caesar. "Et tu, Brute," is as typical of ancient Rome as its conquests.

Among the broken marbles lying in the freshly cut grass is the Arc of Titus, honoring him as the conqueror of Judea. My friend Max Band, the painter, told me a story that might explain why Titus was so honored for conquering such a tiny country and destroying its temple, its spiritual center. According to this legend (or is it history?) the Roman Senate was worried about Judea, a nation which worshipped a powerful God who was invisible; which built a great temple in His name

100

without erecting His image—a God who commanded: "Thou shalt not kill."

An emissary was sent to Judea to learn about these strange people. When he returned, he spoke to the Senate: "A nation," he said, "whose people say 'Peace' when they meet, and 'to life' when they drink is a menace to the great Roman Empire and must be destroyed." The violence of the Romans toward the early Christians—non-violent followers of the Prince of Peace—has the same connotation.

Max Band also told me that he had recently discovered a statement in a tourist guide to the effect that the Colosseum itself was built by Titus "with the sweat and blood of slaves from conquered Judea."

"Imagine," he said, "for 300 lire a guide can show you the ruins of the entire Roman Empire in two hours; but look at what happened to old Judea!"

It is a strange feeling to walk among the ruins of the great Roman Empire a few days after leaving Jerusalem. There are no arches for conquering heroes there but the tomb of King David, the Sanhedrin, the destroyed University on Mount Scopus, the site of learning, guarded day and night behind the walls of old Jerusalem. Outside the walls there is a new University: life and action everywhere. There are ruins all over the Mediterranean coast, ruins of the conquering Romans, just like the ruins in Rome.

There are also monuments, monuments to remember, to honor the victims; *there are none for the conquerors.*

And they say 'peace' when they meet, 'to life' when they drink . . .

* * *

There were drastic changes following the war in June, 1967. It is tragic that Israel, in order to survive, was forced to divert a major part of its energy and resources to military efforts. It can be only hoped that before long it will return again to build a new world, and continue to show what human effort can create if it is used for peace and in the interest of human welfare.

XXXV. ENRICO PACIFICO

We spent the afternoon exploring the narrow streets of the Old City, the small squares with their markets and outdoor trattoria with the inviting aroma from their kitchens, and the profusely inviting gesture of a friendly waiter. Once again we ended up on Piazza Navona, sitting on a bench, watching the fountains, the children, listening to *Arrivederci Roma* coming from the trio in the Tre Scallini resaturant. Here is the unhurried life of Rome, only half an hour's walk from the fashionable Via Veneto, but another world altogether in its atmosphere.

On my first visit to Rome, what had impressed me most had been its magnificent fountains and Michelangelo's *Pietà*. Subsequently, the fountains, lovely as they are, have had to compete for my admiration with many other marvels of the Eternal City, but the *Pietà* still ranks first. The more often I see it, the greater its esthetic and emotional impact. What I feel about this monumental work cannot be understood without reference to the Vatican and the Sistine Chapel. They belong together and beyond their artistic and esthetic value have contributed greatly to my understanding of man's relation to woman, and intimately connected with it to the understanding of Michelangelo, of artist and artistic creations.

Before explaining what I mean, let me tell you something about our present headquarters. We had been unhappy at our hotel. It had been a last-minute reservation made at the height of the tourist season. After a miserable night, we had set out early in the morning for St. Peter's. On foot as usual, we passed a hotel which didn't look like a hotel, just a few minutes' walk from the Cathedral. Marianne, with a gleam in her eye, undeterred by my scepticism, went in to inquire. Presently she emerged and asked whether I would like to see our rooms. Right then and there we hailed a taxi and, after an unpleasant exchange with the manager of the unpleasant hotel, we moved into our new one—into rooms twice the size, half the price and much more to our taste.

Originally, the building had been a monastery but it had long since been converted into a hotel. The walls are thick, the windows solid. There is quiet inside and the noise of the city is muted even with the windows open. Wide corridors lead into large, beautiful panelled halls, some used as dining rooms. Religious paintings, crucifixes in every room, a courtyard with an ancient fountain, early-morning church bells, the rhythmic sound of trotting horses interrupted occasionally by a hoof slipping on the cobblestones like a skipped heartbeat, maintain the illusion that you are living in a monastery and in a time long past.

There are few automobiles on the street but dozens of carriages. Some drivers are busily polishing their carriages or grooming their gentle, patient horses, heads deep in their feed bags. Others are moving to join those already stationed in the great square before St. Peter's—getting into heated gesticulating debates or just snoozing in their high drivers' seats. Priests, usually in pairs, and women in black walk toward the Vatican, bound for Early Mass or to work in the offices and teach in the schools. If I lean out the window, I can see the long slowly rising steps to the entrance of St. Peter's itself and the colorful Swiss guards.

Below me, the basement trattoria is opening its doors. Two young apprentices are washing down the sidewalk and setting up, on the table at the entrance, great baskets of fruit and fresh fish, lobster and scampi decorated with green leaves and colorful vegetables.

It is a pleasant restaurant, frequented by the shopkeepers of the neighborhood, by priests, shy seminary students with their visiting families, Italian tourists and traveling salesmen. We love it. The food is good, the wines exquisite and the waiters friendly. Enthusiastically, they help you select a dozen scampi from the basket and launch into a mouthwatering description of its preparation. All in all, an unusual place to find so near the Vatican, so different from the highly-advertised places overrun by tourists, where you have to empty your pockets as you go through the door. Here, they may look at you sadly if you don't enjoy the food or if they consider your tip inadequate, but their service remains courteous.

They remind me of a driver we once hired in Naples, to take us to Pompeii. He was an attractive, cheerful Sicilian with a

103

lovely name—Enrico Pacifico. He loved his car, his wife, his children and the breathtaking view from the hills of Naples. His fare had been settled in advance.

At the end of the day, as a token of our satisfaction, I gave him what I thought was a large tip. You should have seen his face! He made me feel like a murderer who had not only killed his mother but widowed his wife and was responsible for his hungry orphans. I quickly reached into my pocket to make up for my cruelty, but it took quite a few large Italian notes before his "Grazia, dottore, millegrazia" and his smile compensated me for my empty pockets.

XXXVI. PIETÀ

The Sistine Chapel and Pietà are, above and beyond their artistic value and impact, responsible for my thoughts, my ideas, my understanding of some aspects of man's relation to women.

The first time we saw the Sistine Chapel it was very disappointing. We came on a tour of the Vatican with a sightseeing bus. From the moment we entered the large elevator going up to the Vatican museums, we were pushed through the museum halls full of art treasures one could not see, through narrow corridors and emptied—or rather stuffed—into the chapel in such numbers there was hardly any room to stand. Dozens of guides spoke in monotones to groups of different nationalities: Italian, French, German, English. Their voices blended. The inevitability of listening to all of them at the same time made any attempt at comprehending impossible. It looked like Grand Central Station at the 5 o'clock rush hour, like the departing summercamp groups with their excited group leaders on the first day of school vacation, accompanied by all the parents and relatives not knowing whether they should laugh or cry, enjoy it or be unhappy.

We have been back in the Sistine Chapel many times since, usually at lunch time. For about two hours it is practically empty and those who are there come for the same reason, just to sit silently in a corner, tiptoe from one view to the other, to look, contemplate, enjoy the beauty of it.

104

It was there on one of the visits, admiring the masterpieces of Michelangelo depicting man's fate from creation to damnation, covering the ceiling, the walls, every corner of that beautiful chapel, that I once again heard the voice of the teacher of my childhood, saw the words in the writing of a child, or in the magnificent famous Bibles: God created the Universe.

How many times did I ask questions about that as a child, only to be scorned for asking.

Children ask questions until they are intimidated or learn that it is no use. The adults either don't know the answer or they don't want to give it. People with this kind of experience as children might go through the rest of their lives not asking any more questions, disinterested, or looking for the prophets on earth, especially if the answers of the prophets are simple, black or white, no ifs, no doubts, no questions. They follow leaders who appear to be honest, forthright, free of the trademarks of an intellectual, the scientist who questions, who doubts, who searches for new answers.

You see, we all have been children, we all have been told, we all had the need to believe that adults know everything. According to the era we live in we will be impressed with a great warrior, a great orator, a hero, a great general, a rabble-rouser, who can convince the masses to blame others for their failures, the politician with the mellow voice and with the graying temple.

There are always others—never in the majority—who cannot help asking questions; the odd fellows, the doubters—who cannot sleep because their thoughts drive them to think—who refuse the sleeping pills offered in this era of tranquillizers, refuse in any era simple beliefs, simple answers to the complicated, unanswered questions about life.

From among these doubters throughout history came those men and women who contributed to civilization, to science, to culture, to art; the greatest enemies of tyrants, of the man on the white horse with the simple answers. Even if their answers were not always correct, had to be changed, modified, dis-

105

carded, they ask questions, challenging questions, and they never insisted that they knew all the answers.

Freud was one of those who was forced to ask questions, to try to find answers, who taught us more about human psychology than anyone else. Yet all I learned from him and others in addition to the questions of my childhood—left unanswered by the nuns in a convent, by the Jesuit priests, the protestant or Jewish teachers of my teens—raised one question over and over again—how come?

God created the Universe—so the Genesis teaches us—and as the crowning achievement he created man in his own image and it was good. Man was lonely so God helped him to create out of his own body the first woman!

And there in the Vatican, in the stronghold where man is supreme, where women are banned, sexuality rejected or treated as non-existent, answers came to old questions and new ones, which were so difficult to formulate before.

It gave theoretical answers about the relations between men and women, about Michelangelo. It became natural that if Pietà had to be in St. Peter's, then the story of Genesis had to be painted in the Vatican. They belong together and even if Michelangelo undertook the task with great reluctance, it was natural that he was the one, the creator of Pietà who had to do it.

There in the middle of the ceiling is the magnificent figure of God, that powerful, strong man, the way I visualized Him as a child, and I have seen Him so in dreams as in pictures before I knew of Michelangelo. The figure of the same powerful man Michelangelo created in his Moses.

Here is that magnificent, powerful masculinity creating the sun, the moon, the earth, the ocean, the forests, the billions of living creatures inhabiting the earth and finally, with a touch of his finger, that beautiful young man depicted by Michelangelo. And all this in six days. Yet all this is not complete until he helps *the first man* to perform the miracle of all miracles, to create from his own body, *to give birth to the first woman,* thereby usurping the one function of the woman he is incapable of performing.

106

The answer to this beautiful fantasy must be man's envy of woman's ability to create a new life and his resulting hostility toward her. If there is any validity to this reasoning, then what happens following the creation of the first woman is a logical sequence. In the shortest time, she is depicted as the reason for man's downfall, for his being driven forever from paradise; she is pleasure giving, necessary and the source of all evil. Listen to the words of the *Malleus Malificarum*, The Witches' Hammer, written by two monks of the 16th Century: "What else is woman but a foe to friendship, a desirable calamity, a domestic danger, a delectable detriment, an evil of nature, painted with fair colors."

Below the Sistine Chapel in a niche of St. Peter's Cathedral is Pietà, for me the most beautiful of artistic creations.

The figure of the young, forever young, forever beautiful, idealized, asexual, virgin mother holding the lifeless body of her murdered son in her lap gives answers to the many questions about mother and son, about creation, about man's violence.

Both the youthful Madonna and the body of Jesus are age-less, and either one of them could be exchanged with those of Madonna and the Child, created by Michelangelo a few years before. If Jesus had been killed right after he was born, if she were holding the limp body of the newborn child in her arms, it wouldn't make any difference. The meaning would be the same.

Pietà means sorrow, pity; but pity for whom? Is it for Christ? Possible. Sorrow? Undoubtedly. But the expression on her face, the gesture with her left hand are not expressions of sorrow, of pity alone; they seem to wonder, ask the puzzled question: Why? What's the reason for this? What's the sense in it? Maybe the pity, the sorrow is not just a mother's sorrow for her murdered son, but also her pity for him and *for all men who cannot create, but can only destroy life created by women.*

Michelangelo carved into the ribbon crossing between the breasts of the Madonna: "Michelangelo of Firenze made this." It is a peculiar place for an artist to carve his name and there are all kinds of explanations for it. I would like to give you mine. This was not only the perfect way to express a man's desire to identify with the asexual mother, expressing both the desire and ability to create life just as she can, but also the unconscious expression of the hostility toward her creation resulting in senseless destruction. Yes, this is the compensation a great artist has to make up for man's inability to create life; the explanation for man's greater artistic and scientific creative ability and need.

Michelangelo, the great creative artist, depicted every aspect of man's struggle with his inability to create life. In the paintings covering the walls of the Sistine Chapel is the universal phantasy that not woman but man is the Creator; in Pietà Michelangelo's own unconscious phantasy of creation was expressed by bringing to life that magnificent piece of stone. That is, almost to life, not quite. With all the warmth, with its eternal beauty, its indelible impact, it is still not life, still just a piece of cold, lifeless marble, as cold as the lifeless body of the murdered Christ.

XXXVII. FREUD AND SHAKESPEARE

Psychoanalysts have been interested in all forms of artistic expressions since the beginnings of psychoanalysis.

Freud's interest in literature was not only intense, but also an important source to implement his psychological studies and a medium to demonstrate some of his basic theoretical concepts. He took great pleasure in analyzing, utilizing psychoanalytic knowledge for the understanding of artistic and literary creations. His essays on Leonardo Da Vinci, the Moses of Michelangelo, works of Shakespeare, such as King Lear in the "Theme of the Three Caskets," Ibsen's Rosmersholm, Jensen's Gradiva and others are valuable scientific contributions, and thanks to his own literary ability, delightful reading. The analysis of Hamlet by Ernest Jones, similar works by other analysts are also cornerstones in the understanding of masters and their creations.

But in the beginning, Freud and other psychoanalysts, seeing the clear expression of unconscious drives, conflicts, motivations in literary and other artistic creations, mistook their own understanding of them for the same understanding on the part of the author, the artist. It took time to realize that this was a mistake. For had that been the case, Shakespeare would not have been a great writer, but a great scientist like Freud. There isn't a single human drive, conflict, emotion that cannot be clearly seen in the works of Shakespeare; some of Ibsen's plays could be looked upon as if they would have been the result of psychoanalytic knowledge. But were they?

Dostoyevsky talked about the concept of unconscious guilt long before there was psychoanalysis. But were all these writers aware of the existence, the expressions, the meanings, the content of the unconscious? Of course not. When Jensen was told of Freud's analysis of his Gradiva, he reacted with utter disbelief. Leonardo Da Vinci's artistic creations were in reverse ratio to his scientific interests. One of the prerequisites for artistic creations seems to be lack of awareness of the unconscious motives.

There is another prerequisite: ability, talent or whatever we wish to call it. In order to avoid misunderstandings, it is necessary to state that psychoanalysis learned a great deal about artistic activity and is able to contribute to the understanding of the creative process. Sometimes it can explain the style, the specific form and meaning of an artistic creation. It might elucidate the need, the pressure driving the artist to creative *activity*, or the conflicts which interfere with it, but psychoanalysis does not claim to know, to explain *artistic ability, creative talent*. Many tried, but no one ever explained a genius.

There are important and interesting studies about great creative minds in the fields of science, art and literature. They were studied by historians, biographers, and many of them by psychoanalysts.

We learned a great deal about their lives, their struggles, hopes and pleasures, about their achievements and failures, their realistic and neurotic difficulties.

But regardless how interesting, enjoyable or valuable these studies might be, they do not give any explanation of their creative ability.

109

My personal interest in art and literature dates back to the earliest years of my life when I was fortunate to be exposed to the great artistic collections, to the paintings, sculptures, the music of the masters in the Catholic church in Europe, alternating with the haunting melodies of orthodox Jewish ceremonies. My life-long interest in the theatre, in the performing arts and artists dates back also to the religious plays, the pageantry, the ceremonies observed and participated in in the nursery school of a convent, even though my stage activities did not go beyond one appearance representing a palm—not even a tree, just a branch! But my attraction to art, my pleasure, my interest to understand, to promote art and culture never diminished. On the contrary, it increased with every year, every decade, every war.

In order to demonstrate psychoanalytic concepts of artistic creations, let me tell you something about my understanding of Hamlet and Cleopatra as seen by Shakespeare and Bernard Shaw, and the analysis of King Lear by Freud.

Hamlet is one of the most universally liked Shakespearean characters. If we ask the question why, we get all kinds of answers.

He was very kind, we hear, but was he? He was a devoted son—loved his mother, loved Ophelia,—but did he only love them?

And so the explanations go, but obviously none of them is satisfactory.

Ernest Jones, noted British psychoanalyst, wrote the only major psychoanalytic study of Hamlet. His emphasis is on the vicissitudes of the Oedipus Complex; the universal conflict of all boys in the process of maturation, the forbidden incestuous wish toward the mother and the guilt over the destructive, hostile wishes toward the father.

Shakespeare's Hamlet demonstrates this conflict in all its aspects almost as clearly as the Oedipus Trilogy by Sophocles. Yet I do not believe that it explains the universal empathy.

To me, Hamlet represents the total picture of the human struggle for maturation. He is the helpless little boy, who is the center of interest, but at the same time is neglected, excluded from the life of the adults. He is also a big boy who should know how to dress, and how to take care of himself, but frequently he doesn't. He expresses every struggle a child has with the powerful feelings of love and hate. He expresses primarily love for his idealized dead father, hate for the living uncle-father; love for the idealized pure mother, and hate for the feared, desired sexual one.

Only the genius of Shakespeare could have created a character like Hamlet, whose struggle demonstrates ambivalence so richly.

Hamlet represents the struggle of the first years of life, a struggle that repeats itself during puberty with even greater intensity. He expresses the conflicts as we experience it for the third time at the end of the adolescent years, during the final struggle of separation from infantile attachments, on the road to achieving and accepting manhood.

"To be or not to be" is usually understood in terms of life or death. Impressive as it is, it cannot be the only question, the only conflict. The "question" has to be continued: to be or not to be—what? A child or an adult, loving or hating, constructive or destructive, like father or like uncle, or like mother, a man or a woman, a failure or a success, powerful or helpless, great or nothing, sexual or intellectual, dirty or clean. What am I? What can I be? What do I want to be?

We see the resentment toward duties and responsibilities, shame and guilt about pleasure and desires, regardless of whether they are experienced in reality or remain forever just phantasy. Yet even all this would not explain the universal liking for Hamlet. There is one added absolutely essential requirement to mobilize the universal empathy; namely, *he is and he has to be a failure* in the struggle of maturation. Would he evoke the same liking if he had killed just the one man—the usurper of the throne, the "incestuous" sexual partner of his mother; if he had become the king?! If he had been successful in sexual maturation by marrying a loving and loved Ophelia or any other eligible, attractive young lady of the court or

111

even if he simply had enjoyed a love affair? He had to be a failure, destroying everything he could have been, everyone whom he loved and hated, and, with them, himself.

He could be the "Sweet Prince" only when he was dead. Alive he would have been just another king, another tyrant, usurping the throne by killing his father's killer, striking terror in the hearts of his subjects. As just an ordinary man, an ordinary fate, who would have cared? As a truly great one, he would have been loved by some, hated by many, envied probably by all.

* * *

A young student of literature asked me once whether I considered Cleopatra a cruel and destructive woman. At first I was puzzled, but then it became clear that coming from a student of literature it was a perfectly resonable question.

Cleopatra was obviously an intriguing woman. Otherwise she would not have attracted so much attention.

Historians and writers have seen her according to their own tastes, their own attitudes toward women. The spectrum ranges from an envious, jealous, immature, scheming, unreliable sex fiend to a mature, clever, thinking, unhappy, betrayed and misused woman. The first description is more prevalent.

Cleopatra has always impressed me as a mature woman and I have always liked her. She must have been very beautiful, a woman who was aware of being desired by men and as seductive as women should be if they are not afraid of attracting men.

She was accused of being greedy for power, wanting to be unquestioned ruler of Egypt, to take the crown away from her brother out of sheer jealousy. As a woman, she was accused of using her sexual attraction to blackmail Caesar, to destroy all men in her life, —her brother, Caesar, Mark Anthony, —and to be willing to sacrifice her dynasty and Egypt to her insatiable quest for power.

Somehow this story has never appealed to me. Of course she was ambitious. What else could we expect of anyone with her background and position? Undoubtedly she wanted to take the crown away from her brother and she could have done it with-

112

out the help of Caesar. But maybe she did not do all this out of craving for power alone, but also in the interest of Egypt. Her brother, according to available accounts, could not be considered a very bright, gifted or impressive person. Since the male members of her dynasty could not produce even a King Faruk, she was the only hope of saving Egypt from total destruction.

Yet, have we ever heard of women getting credit for achievements in history? Ever since Eve, women have been blamed for men's failure. They were considered the source of all evil. And so was Cleopatra. History, we must remember, was written almost exclusively by men and I am not aware of any female contributors to the Book of Books.

Man's ambivalence to woman, with various degrees of hostility, ranging from mistrust to outright hatred, is more prevalent than we care to admit. And toward successful, powerful, beautiful women it is of course even stronger.

If you read both Shakespeare and Shaw on Cleopatra, you will learn a great deal about Cleopatra, but even more about Shakespeare and Shaw.

Let us take Shakespeare's Cleopatra first. It is by far the more impressive. Shakespeare presents a mature woman of about middle age (she was supposed to be about 28 years old at the beginning of her love affair with Anthony).

"My salad days when I was green in judgment," is a line that could have come only from a mature person. A woman of great beauty, pride and power, devoted to her family background, to Egypt, yielding to the man she loves, capable of the mature person's wide range of emotions, from love to jealousy to hate, from mistrust to doubt to devotion. Queen on the throne, unquestioned master to her subjects, she is the Goddess of sexuality in the arms of her lover. A complete being with her pleasures and pain, with successes and failures, the perfect and the imperfect human, Shakespeare was able to create so masterfully.

Whether he created a character of fantasy, or used historical figures, whether he described a beggar, a common soldier, a servant or a king, he humanized them. He stripped them of the

113

artificial cloak of greatness, put on them by their subjects or by history to idolize them, to make them fit subjects for a glory they did not have, for deification frequently far beyond their own need or desire.

Still he never took away their dignity.

On the contrary, he endowed them with the dignity of human strength and weakness, making it possible for everyone to understand them, to identify with them in their hopes, in their struggles, pleasures and pains.

He sent only one message: the human body, the human spirit, in its beauty and ugliness, with its pleasure and its suffering.

His characters never lost their style in success or in adversity; they are always identifiable. Cleopatra, for example, can love and hate, go through every emotion human beings are capable of. Her actions are kind or cruel, but she remains always Cleopatra, the unquestioned true daughter of the generous, life-giving, powerful, unconquerable Queen: the Nile.

Only a mature, self-sacrificing woman could utter the words of the dying Cleopatra while offering her breast to the fangs of the serpent: "Like the babe that sucks the nurse to sleep." This is how Shakespeare presented her—at least to me. Obviously I do not consider her only cruel and destructive.

Compare with that the Cleopatra of Shaw. He did not choose the Cleopatra at the height of her maturity, but the Cleopatra who enters history with the arrival of Julius Caesar. His Cleopatra is a narcissistic, unreliable, peacock-brained, cuddly little Egyptian kitten, her sharp claws in soft paws always ready to scratch if you don't watch out. All in all, a helpless little thing, whom Caesar tries to teach something. She has the shifting insensitivity and identity of an adolescent girl, pre-occupied more with her looks than anything else, a not very impressive figure with little substance and not much future. The description might better fit a fantasy about an adolescent Irish lass, than the sensual, rapidly maturing daughter of the Pharaoh, who lived in a land where at the age of 12 to 13 girls normally are mature women. And due to her status, of course, Cleopatra undoubtedly was treated from early childhood with the reverence, respect and adoration due to only a select few throughout history.

The answer to the two different Cleopatras is the obvious difference between Shakespeare and Shaw. As I said before, Shakespeare humanized his characters, made them accessible and understandable, brought them near to us. A man can do that only if he is capable of accepting himself with all human limitations, a man capable of permitting himself the enjoyment of the pleasures of life. Such a man, liking people in general, can permit himself to see all sides of them, the good without envy, the bad with understanding and tolerance, without exaggeration.

Shaw was a satirist. He was intolerant of himself and of others. Judging from his works and utterances, he must have disliked people in general and women in particular, looking for and finding the weak points for his ridicule, scorn, righteous indignation. Regardless of how delightful his style, how great his literary ability, how impressive his social messages, his characters are one-sided, exaggerated caricatures of total human beings.

His fear and dislike of women must have been great. One of the few female figures he ever glorified was Joan of Arc. She was an immature girl, rejecting and rebelling against everything resembling femininity, fighting with men against men, until finally she was burned at the stake. She ended her life the untouchable, untouched, non-sexual virgin, without any possibility of developing into a woman; her body untouched by the flame of passion was consumed by the fire of hate.

As a final word about Cleopatra, I must add that I really never could understand Anthony and Cleopatra without the knowledge of the relationship of both of them to Julius Caesar.

Caesar and Anthony were two generations of men, almost like father and son, with all the devotion, affection, jealousy and competition characteristic of that kind of relationship.

Cleopatra was the beautiful, sensuous, powerful lover of both, the connecting link between the two generations. It is no mere coincidence that, after the murder of Julius Caesar, Anthony never became his rightful successor, even though realistically it was entirely up to him. Anthony became the lover, married Cleopatra, the wife of his great predecessor. He was humiliated, defeated, ridiculed by those whom he could have ruled, dying finally by his own hand exactly the same way as the real killers of the Ides of March ended their lives after being hunted down by Anthony, the avenger of Julius Caesar. Retribution for the unconscious guilt of the oedipal struggle is clearly recognizable and undeniable.

I just remembered that you asked me whether I could explain the difference between Cleopatra and Lady Macbeth. If I use what I learned both from Freud and Shakespeare I might be able to do so; if I do not succeed, it won't be their fault.

If Cleopatra is the successful, mature, loving, warm, voluptuous, fertile, desirable woman, then Lady Macbeth is the unsuccessful, regressed, immature, dried up, cold, barren, unattractive and undesirable woman, her life dominated by insatiable, greedy hunger for power, by envy, by murderous hatred and devastating guilt. Cleopatra is longing for motherhood; Lady Macbeth is hating it. Remember the Nile scene and the subsequent change in Cleopatra's relationship? Her personality? If we use the river as the symbolic representation of mother and motherhood, then we could say that Cleopatra, emerging from her symbolic identification with mother Nile, grew from adolescent girlhood into full, ripe womanhood.

The Nile was worshipped throughout history as the powerful, life-giving, fertile mother, creating, embracing, feeding Egypt under the warm, brilliant Mediterranean sun.

If the Nile is the model for Cleopatra's womanhood, what should we choose for Lady Macbeth? A dried-up desert river? No. The desert is hot and, even if it cannot quench our thirst, it is full of life. It would have to be a frozen, shallow creek, somewhere in the north of the British Isles, covered with shifting dense fog, driven by the bone-chilling, icy winds of the North Sea, where roaming wild beasts, driven by hunger, howl with pain when their hot, thirsty tongues get caught, burned by the deceiving, glittering ice.

116

Even in her death, Cleopatra, offering her full life and pleasure-giving breast, to the poisonous fangs of the snake, remains the giving, sacrificing mother. Encased in her magnificent, protecting tomb, she returns, reunites with the eternal mother of the warm Egyptian soil, the creation of the blessed Nile she emerged from.

Now listen to Lady Macbeth reproaching her husband for hesitating to kill Duncan, the King:
"I have given suck, and know how tender 'tis to love the babe that milks me: I would, while it was smiling in my face, have pluck'd my nipple from his boneless gums, and dash'd the brains out, had I so sworn as you have done to this."

There is only one more aspect of this that I would like to mention. It helps to explain the impact Shakespearean characters have on us.

Looking at the contrast between Cleopatra and Lady Macbeth, we have to understand them also as the external pictures of our own shifting ambivalence toward women, the image of the loving and hating, but also the loved and hated mother.

You will find many expressions of this in the works of Shakespeare. The one coming to mind at once is King Lear with his three daughters. What a contrast among Goneril, Regan and Cordelia!

Most of the works of Shakespeare can be used for studies ranging from the use of words to deepest psychological meanings; his characters have been explained by writers, critics, and recreated on the stage in an endless variety. And rightly so. Interpretation of an action and the understanding of a character has many different meanings. Although one can argue, agree or disagree with different interpretations, that doesn't necessarily mean that one is right, the others wrong. Even if explanations appear sometimes to be absolutely contradictory, they both can be correct. One of the characteristics of the human mind is that totally contradictory drives and forces can exist simultaneously. Whatever I say or quote from Freud about Lear should be understood with this in mind.

I have heard many explanations, seen different interpretations on the stage, with good and bad acting, with emphasis on one or the other of the endless possibilities.

Remember what I told you about Hamlet? If he portrayed the identity struggle of the late adolescent ending in total failure, then King Lear represents an old man's struggle with, and acceptance of, the inevitability of death.

Let me tell you first of Freud's ideas about Lear and death and, I will tell you about some of my own thoughts about both.

Whenever possible I will quote Freud verbatim. His language is so beautiful and so concise that it would be a shame to paraphase.

Freud says: "To avoid misunderstandings, I should like to say that it is not my purpose to deny that King Lear's dramatic story is intended to inculcate two wise lessons: that one should not give up one's possessions and rights during one's lifetime, and that one must guard against accepting flattery at its face value... Yet it seems to me quite impossible to explain the overpowering effect of King Lear from the impressions that such a train of thought would produce or to suppose that the dramatist's personal motives did not go beyond the intention of teaching these lessons."

In order to arrive at his conclusions, he starts out with the "... scenes in the suitor's choice between the three caskets in the Merchant of Venice. The caskets of gold, silver and lead." Using mythology, psychoanalytic knowledge and understanding of symbolism and dreams, Freud comes to the conclusion that the three "caskets are also women, symbols of what is essential in woman herself—like coffers, boxes, cases, baskets, and so on... and now we see that the theme is a human one, a man's choice between three women."

Freud then goes on to show how frequently this choice repeats itself in mythology, in fairy tales and ..."that the third of the three women is the most desirable, the best, and mos. reliable. Furthermore, indications would lead us to conclude that the third one of the sisters between whom the choice is made is a dead woman. But she may be something else as well —namely, Death itself, the Goddess of Death."

"Lear is an old man," Freud says. "It is for this reason, as we

118

have already said, that the three sisters appear as his daughters ... But Lear is not only an old man, he is a dying man ... But the doomed man is not willing to renounce the love of women; he insists on hearing how much he is loved. Do you remember the moving final scene, one of the culminating points of tragedy in modern dramas. Lear carries Cordelia's dead body onto the stage. Cordelia is Death. If we reverse the situation it becomes intelligible and familiar to us. She is the Death-Goddess who, like the Valkyrie in German mythology, carries away the dead hero from the battle-field. Eternal wisdom, clothed in the primeval myths, bids the old man renounce love, choose death and make friends with the necessity of dying."

Freud concludes: "We might argue that what is represented here are the three inevitable relations that a man has with a woman—the woman who bears him, the woman who is his mate and the woman who destroys him; or that they are the three forms taken by the figure of the mother in the course of a man's life—the mother herself, the beloved one who is chosen after her pattern, and lastly the Mother Earth who receives him once more. But it is in vain that an old man yearns for the love of woman as he had it first from his mother; the third of the Fates alone, the silent Goddess of Death, will take him into her arms."

The temptation to leave Freud's beautiful words without comment is great, yet he was the last one to expect that and the first one to drive ahead, urging others to do the same, to look, to search, and to widen the understanding of human psychology.

In view of these later understandings, it is justifiable to add that in death, through reunion with Mother Earth, the ambivalent struggle of love and hate toward mother, is eliminated. A non-ambivalent oneness with the love one is re-established.

Therefore one could look upon this reunion as a denial of the existence of ambivalence and a denial of death itself.

Freud in his paper: Thoughts on War and Death, says, "The tendency to exclude death from our calculations brings in its train a number of other renunciations and exclusions ... It is an inevitable result of all this that we should seek in the

119

world of fiction, of general literature and of the theatre compensation for the improverishment of life There we still find people who know how to die, indeed, who are even capable of killing someone else. There alone too we can enjoy the condition which makes it possible for to reconcile ourselves with death—namely, that behind all the vicissitudes of life, we preserve our existence intact . . . In the realm of fiction we discover that plurality of lives for which we crave. We die in the person of a given hero, yet we survive him, and are ready to die again with the next hero just as safely."

The struggle of accepting and denying death is represented in a variety of ways in King Lear. In the mad scene, for example, it is expressed in a dream-like form, with all the distortions and symbolism characteristic of dreams, Lear, naked, disheveled, his hair, his body covered with flowers, offering food to the birds, with no food in his extended hand, represents both death and the connection, the continuation of death in new life.

People are at first puzzled when I talk about the denial of death. After all—they say—how can one deny death. We see it, experience it, live with it constantly; the murders, the accidents, the wars, the quiet departing of small children before they can become aware of life at all, and the old ones leaving behind new generations they created, are part of daily life. Yet in spite of all, can you visualize being dead? No, there are certain things the human mind is incapable of concaptualizing; such as, infinity, timelessness and death. We can talk about it, create mathematical formulas, explain the chemical, physical aspects of it. That is our limit. But we cannot think of our own death without being also the observer.

Remember when you were a little child? Sometimes, when your feelings were hurt, you were angry at your parents. How painfully delicious it was to daydream about being dead, drowned, falling out of a tall tree. And the beautiful funeral! There they were: your parents, your brothers and sisters, even your favorite pooch, crying, suffering . . . It was so real, so touching, that it brought tears to your eyes watching them!

What about the powerful old patriarchs—and matriarchs—

who make wills giving them more power over generations yet unborn than they had during their own lifetime. No, they do not accept death. They continue living and with these carefully drawn, iron-clad trust funds they tell *you* how to live, what is good for you or else.

And what about religions? Ancient, primitive, Christian, Jewish, Oriental? Life after death, whether in heaven or in hell, is eternal.

Some live with the fear of death throughout life. Their fears sometimes reach proportions of such intensity that they die a thousand deaths, their terror never leaving them. Others accept the reality of natural death, do not live with anxiety about it and are capable of dying peacefully, without anger, without rebellion.

Yes, as Freud says: "External wisdom ... bids the old man renounce love ... make friends with the necessity of dying."

Let me bring you back to Hamlet for a moment. For him to accept death at his age represents total failure in his struggle for identity. Hamlet's life lay ahead of him; Lear's behind him. Success for a young man is rejection of death and an acceptance of manhood; for an old man success is the acceptance of the inevitability of the end of life.

King Lear dies at the end peacefully in the arms of his beloved and only loving daughter. He dies as an understanding wise man, having gone through the identity struggle of an old man. His peaceful acceptance of death is the victory, the only victory possible in old age.

It should be possible to come to this conclusion easier and earlier than Lear did. The prerequisite for it is a life in which we can love others, not just ourselves, in which we are capable of receiving love from others without fear, accept every age with its advantages and disadvantages, privileges and limitations.

Paris, Orly Airport

XXXVIII. GOING HOME.

We are homeward bound at last. We left Rome early in the afternoon and are now at Orly Airport, outside Paris, where we must change planes for Los Angeles. It is raining hard and we have just been informed that our plane has been delayed for several hours.

We have finished shopping at this duty-free airport for the last silk blouses, bottles of perfume, Cointreau, Armagnac and Napoleon brandy—and now we feel keenly the impatience and restlessness so typical at the end of every journey. All at once you realize how tired you are and you long for the most comfortable bed in all the world, your own. You can't wait to be home again, where you can walk around in the dark, know every flower in the garden, miss every branch the gardener cut off while you were gone.

The wait for the flight to Los Angeles seems endless. The excitement through weeks of travel by plane, train, car, on foot, has subsided and you are suspended in space and time. There is no way back and just one way out—by the plane you are waiting for.

"Attention, passengers . . ." The loudspeaker announces departures to every part of the world. You watch a group get up, walk to a gate with embarcation cards in hand, but they are just strangers bound for strange places. The only announcement that counts is the one you are still awaiting, the departure for Los Angeles.

After a while the resentment at the delay disappears. Your thoughts reach out beyond the flight to all the things that home represents, to the routine of life interrupted completely so many weeks ago. Glancing at my family, I am sure they

122

too are now looking ahead to the activities, duties and pleasures of the next days and months.

One thought I know we are all sharing at this moment—the joy of seeing Fifi again. Fifi is our miniature French poodle, as much a member of the family as only a poodle can be. She is the latest and dearest addition to our home, following Tom and Jerry, our black and white spaniels, the 27 guinea pigs, the tame and wild birds, frogs, turtles and other survivors of Noah's Ark which have inhabited our home over the years.

Fifi was about eight weeks old when we all fell in love with her at first sight. That was more than ten years ago. From the very first, she was a source of joy. Her intelligence, her personality, her disposition are beyond description. I have never heard her growl. She had a kissing relationship with the more intelligent guinea pigs; she learned to dislike cats only because they run away, refuse to play, refuse to become friends. She loves to catch snails for Marianne and it isn't her fault that these pesky creatures sometimes hid in the branches of delicate, breakable plants.

"If you love her so, how could you bear to leave her behind for so long a time?" I hear you ask. A justifiable question. The answer is that though some European countries welcome pets (in many restaurants a poodle gets a chair at the table)—there are others, like England, which have a strict quarantine. But there is an even more important reason why we cannot travel with her. When she was about two years old, we discovered that she was suffering from a congenital defect common to poodles, affecting both hind legs. Her kneecaps slipped out when she stood up and her legs collapsed.

After a while she couldn't walk and had to have a series of operations which enabled her finally to use one hind leg but not the other. Even though she can run around the garden, chasing birds or unsociable cats, she tires easily and has to be carried much of the time. It is a comfort to us and to her that she is boarding with the nurse who took care of her in the hospital where she had her operations. She not only sleeps in the same bed with the nurse and her husband, but even has a small Yorkshire Terrier for company. We are almost afraid she may not be satisfied with just ourselves as sleeping companions.

Fifi's bad knees are also the reason why we could not breed her. It would have been too difficult for her and chances are that her puppies would have inherited the defect. It is a pity; she would make a wonderful mother. She has never had a false pregnancy, quite common among poodles, but for a few years she has done something that is a delight to watch.

Five or six weeks after being in season, she *plays* mother. Among the birthday presents she has received from our equally pet-devoted friends are three squeaking rubber dolls—a dog angel, a hippopotamus and an elephant. These are her favorite toys, carefully kept together next to the fireplace. She selects one or the other to play with, delighting in their particular squeaks.

During her fantasied motherhood, the three of them become her puppies. She tries to pick them up carefully so they will not squeak, carries one after the other to our bed, asking to be helped up. (It is difficult for her to jump and she wouldn't anyway, while carrying her puppies.) Then she lays them down together in a fold of the blanket, licks them clean and wakes up immediately during the night if for some reason one or the other would squeak. Whenever she has to relieve herself, she takes them with her into the garden, then brings them back to our bed or to a comfortable chair.

This goes on for three or four weeks. When she decides that they are old enough, she starts playing rough with them, making them squeak more than ever. Then, once again, they become just toys to play with until the next time. Of course all three of them are with her in her adopted home while we are gone.

When Fifi was a puppy and actually until she had her operations, she slept in her own bed in the kitchen. We used to bed her down, give her her rag doll with the chewed-up nose, cover her up and she would go to sleep. But after her first operation all that changed. She spent a week in the hospital with a heavy splint on her leg, lost half her weight, became severely depressed and started biting the attendants.

After her subsequent operations, we brought her home im-

124

mediately when she started coming out of the anesthesia. One of us sat beside her during the day, feeding her sips of chicken broth or ice cream. At night, she slept beside Marianne. The smell of ether was so strong that after a while Marianne was ready for an operation herself.

Fifi was never depressed again, nor did she ever move back to her own bed. Gradually, for longer and longer periods, she moved into our bed and by now she is a permanent fixture. She goes to the children's beds in the morning to wake them up or to catch a few extra winks while Marianne is fixing breakfast.

It is good to look forward to her greeting. She will cry all the way home. Then she will go out into the garden, her jungle world where she is absolute master, check every brush, follow every scent of the frogs, lizards and neighborhood cats who will have taken advantage of her absence to roam unmolested, fight their mighty love fights and chase after birds. She will stand in the middle of the garden and bark—at no one in particular—just to let everyone, friends and foe, know that she is back.

Above all, I look forward to returning to my office, to my patients: those who will be glad to see me back and those who will express resentment that I "abandoned" them. Some will express their anger directly, without hesitation. Others will say I needn't have come back—that not only did they not miss me but that they felt much better while I was gone. Still others will relate in detail and with more or less anxiety all the airplane crashes, auto accidents and train wrecks they heard about while I was gone.

"I couldn't help thinking of you each time . . . But why should I have cared . . . I'm sure you never thought of me once."

"I wish," one will say, "you would please tell that female who precedes me to stop using that horrible perfume. She stinks up the entire room and my wife accuses me of cheating when she smells it on me."

Or . . . "Oh, I know I owe you some money but there was no point in sending it while you were away. You couldn't use it and your bank certainly didn't need it. Of course you must be completely broke by now, throwing my hard-earned money around, bringing all those expensive presents to *other people* ... Well, I'll bring a check when I get around to it."

Or I will hear from a fearful new patient, yearning for help yet sorry he ever called for an appointment: "I really don't know why I wanted to see you; I can't think of anything to talk about."

And so it goes, not only each time an analyst takes a vacation but during the entire course of an analysis. The agonizing struggle with feelings of anxiety, hate, anger, love and fear ... dredging up painful childhood memories, expectations, disappointments, pleasures. And the work goes on ... human beings struggling to learn what forces in themselves drive them to be fearful, angry, guilt-ridden beyond reason; why they cannot find a mate although they long for one; why they are destructive toward themselves and others though they don't want to be; why they rebel against or submit to authorities existing only in their fantasies; why they are so terrified of loneliness, of the ghosts that haunt them by night and by day.

It takes a great deal of courage to overcome the anxiety and shame most patients feel in seeking the help of a psychoanalyst. What with all the "sophisticated" jokes, wisecracks and bravado which surround the subject, most patients would prefer any physical illness however severe or crippling to being labelled "weak" or "sick in the head."

Yes, it takes courage and should command respect for those who struggle day after day to face themselves, to see themselves and the rest of humanity as they really are, not as they think they ought to be ... to develop the strength to grow and to throw off the chains that bind them to the terrors of the long forgotten past.

It takes a long time to learn that adults have choices ... that "what you don't know won't hurt you" is false, that exactly the opposite is true. It takes even longer to realize that one's Unconscious is not all hell, all bad ... that everything creative in human beings, everything that is pleasurable, beautiful and valuable also has roots in the Unconscious.

Yes, I am eager to get back to work, to be in my quiet office again, behind my cluttered desk, and to rest my eyes once more on my lovely pictures by Max Band.

One is a charcoal sketch of the biblical Deluge, the face of Noah, tense and troubled . . . the placid, wide-eyed animals . . . the turbulent sea . . . the rainbow . . . the first rays of the sun breaking through and a dove bearing an olive branch.

Another is a gouache of a flowering peach orchard, bursting with life and color. And between the two is one of my prize possessions, a painting of Jeremiah in subtle, exquisite tones of rust-red and green. The head of the prophet, supported by his hand, expresses with overwhelming impact man's eternal weariness, mature contemplation and quiet despair.

"Attention, passengers- Flight # . . . non-stop to Los Angeles is now ready for boarding at Gate . . . s'il vous plait . . ."